DANCE
EXAMINATIONS
BOARD

Latin American
Cha Cha Cha

THE IMPERIAL SOCIETY OF TEACHERS OF DANCING
IMPERIAL HOUSE, 22/26 PAUL STREET
LONDON EC2A 4QE
TELEPHONE NO: 020 7377 1577   FAX NO: 020 7247 8979

e-mail:sales@istd.org
website:http://www.istd.org

Issued by the

Latin American Dance Faculty Committee

Original published in separate parts between
July 1971 and July 1973

First Edition (5000 copies) July 1974
Second Edition revised and enlarged (4000 copies) 1975
Third Edition revised and enlarged (5000 copies) 1978
Fourth Edition revised and enlarged (3000 copies) 1981
Fifth Edition enlarged (2000 copies) 1983
Sixth Edition revised Part 2 Cha Cha Cha (4000 copies) 1999
Sixth Edition revised Part 2 Cha Cha Cha reprinted with amendments 2003

FIGURES

FOREWORD

The book you are about to read was compiled by the Latin American Dance Faculty committee of the Imperial Society of Teachers of Dancing, their experience covering every facet of teaching from the beginner and medal-list to the competitor and professional examination candidate. This is a book for teachers by teachers, and is a reference book to enable teachers to develop the rhythm and character of the dances in their pupils at all levels.

A close study of our leading Latin exponents, past and present, was carried out and every modern development considered.

Figures have been added to the syllabus according to popularity, and the existing technique has been clarified, resulting in an easy to read analysis in chart form.

It will be noted from the Latin American syllabus that the figures for the professional candidate have been carefully graded to the consistent with those of the medallist. For example, in the theoretical section the Student - Teacher is required to have knowledge of the figures best suited to beginners, social dancing and the Social Dance Tests. The Associate syllabus embraces the Bronze medal figures, Licentiate the Silver, and Fellow the Gold. However, in the practical demonstration section of the professional examinations candidates may include figures from the next level in their dancing if they wish, although no technical questions will be asked on these figures. For example, the Student - Teacher may dance figures from the Associate syllabus while the Associate may use figures from the Licentiate and the Licentiate from the Fellowship syllabus.

Teachers are reminded to read the interesting "developments" of some of the figures listed at a lower level; knowledge of these developments will be required for the higher examinations.

This is the official Latin American Technique book upon which the Imperial Society examinations are based. Please refer to the syllabus for further requirements.

Note for teachers who are coaching couples for Juvenile or Novice competitions held under B.D.C. rules. Please refer to the Rule Book published by the British Dance Council for the list of figures and holds allowed for these grades.

ABBREVIATIONS USED IN THIS BOOK

L	Left
R	Right
LF	Left Foot
RF	Right Foot
LOD	Line of Dance
DW	Diagonally to Wall
DC	Diagonally to centre
B	Ball of foot
H	Heel
T	Toe
WF	Whole foot
IE	Inside edge
Fwd	Forward
Bwd	Backward
Diag	Diagonally
PP	Promenade Position
CPP	Counter Promenade Position
LSP	Left Side Position
RSP	Right Side Position
TP	Tandem Position
St	Student - Teacher
A	Associate
L	Licentiate
F	Fellow

Professional Candidates   Please note it is better not to use abbreviations verbally.

PLEASE READ THESE PAGES BEFORE PROGRESSING TO CHARTS

TIME SIGNATURE	4/4 (4 beats to a bar of music)
ACCENT	There is a musical accent on the first beat of each bar, with a percussive accent on the fourth beat of each bar
BEAT VALUE OF EACH STEP (unless otherwise stated)	Count '2' - 1 beat. Count '3' - 1 beat. Count '4' - half beat. Count 'and' - half beat. Count '1' - 1 beat.
TEMPO	30 bars per minute (The speed at which the music is played)
	The tempo given is as required by the British Dance Council for Championships. Slight deviations are acceptable for examinations and tests

NORMAL HOLD AND POISE

Stand with feet apart, facing partner about 15cms (6 inches) apart, with the head erect, the body naturally upright and the shoulders down

The Man's right hand is placed on the Lady's left shoulder blade and the Lady's left arm rests lightly on his right arm following the curve of his arm to the shoulder. The Man's left hand is raised in a gentle curve to the level of the eyes. The Lady's right hand is placed in the Man's left hand with her fingers between his thumb and first finger. The hands are lightly clasped

BODY POSITIONS AND HOLDS USED IN CHA CHA CHA

These refer to the Lady's position in relation to the Man and should be stated prior to giving Foot Positions or a description. Where necessary, for clarity, reference is made to a Body Position in the Foot Position column

1   **CLOSED POSITION (St,A,L&F)**
     Facing partner, slightly apart, normal hold

     Alternative holds

     1   Left hand holding Lady's right hand
     2   Right hand holding Lady's left hand
     3   No hold
     The couple may be a little further apart than usual when using these alternatives

4

2   CONTACT POSITION (L&F)

Facing partner with light body contact and normal hold

3   OPEN POSITION (A,L&F)

Facing and away from partner, approximately at arms length. Left hand holding Lady's right hand

Alternative holds
1   Right hand holding Lady's right hand
2   No Hold
3   Left hand holding Lady's right hand and right hand holding Lady's left hand. (Double Hold)

4   FAN POSITION (A,L&F)

Lady at a 90° angle to Man on his left side on an imaginary line about 15cms (6 inches) in front of him. Left hand holding Lady's right hand. Man's feet apart, weight on RF, Lady LF back, weight on LF

5   PROMENADE POSITION (L&F)

Lady on Man's right side with the Man's right and Lady's left side towards each other, slightly apart, and the opposite side of the body turned outwards to form the shape of a 'V'. Normal hold

6   OPEN PROMENADE POSITION (St,A,L&F)

As Promenade Position with the following holds. The distance apart may vary considerably and become more open, depending on the figure danced
Holds
1   Right hand holding Lady's left hand
2   Left hand holding Lady's right hand
3   No hold

7   OPEN COUNTER PROMENADE POSITION (St,A,L&F)

Lady on Man's left side with Man's left side and Lady's right side towards each other, slightly apart, and the opposite side of the body turned outwards to form the shape of a 'V'. The distance apart may vary considerably and become more open, depending on the figure danced
Holds
1   Left hand holding Lady's right hand
2   No hold

8   **RIGHT SIDE POSITION (St,A,L&F)**

Lady on Man's right side, both facing the same way. Hold as required for figure used

9   **LEFT SIDE POSITION (St,A,L&F)**

Lady on Man's left side, both facing the same way. Hold as required for figure used

10   **TANDEM POSITION (L&F)**

Lady directly in front or behind Man, both facing the same way

11   **RIGHT SHADOW POSITION (F)**

Lady on Man's right side, slightly in advance or slightly behind the Man, both facing the same way. Hold will depend on the figure danced

12   **LEFT SHADOW POSITION (F)**

Lady on Man's left side, slightly in advance or slightly behind the Man, both facing the same way. Hold will depend on the figure danced

USE OF ARMS

The arms are held in a natural and unaffected way. In many figures the partner is held with only one hand and in some cases there is no hold. The free arms are never static.

Movement of the arms is subtle and rhythmically co-ordinated with the movement of the body allowing for personal expression

HIP MOVEMENTS

SIMPLE DEFINITION (St,A,L&F)

Every step commences to move with a slightly flexed knee. On steps taking a full beat of music the knee straightens just before it reaches its position. As weight is taken fully on to the step the hips move naturally in the direction of the leg receiving the weight. The action used on counts "4 and" is described in the Cha Cha Cha Chasse section

OTHER TECHNICAL DEFINITIONS (A.L&F)

1	**SETTLING**	The body weight is settled over a straight standing leg which commences the hip movement. (Used to commence movement of the body weight)
2	**LATERAL**	The hips move to left or right with minimal rotation. (As step 2 of chasse to Left or Right)
3	**ROTATIONAL**	The hips rotate around the vertical line of the spinal column. (Occurs in varying degrees throughout)
4	**TWISTING**	An action where the turn commences in the hips only. (Example Lady's Hip Twists)

A natural, upright position of the body is maintained at all times

RHYTHMIC EXPRESSION (St,A,L&F)

The knee and hip action used on forward or backward steps danced on beats 2 or 3 is similar to Rumba, although, because of the faster tempo, it is completed fractionally later on a forward step taken on beat 2 when followed by a backward step, or on a backward step taken on beat 2 when followed by a forward step. When dancing, for example, the first or sixth step of the Basic Movement it is useful to count '2 and a', completing the action during the last part of the beat on the 'a' count

Although the first step of each figure is taken on the second beat of music (count 2) the dance is commenced with the hips already moving on the preceding beats 4 1. This is normally achieved by taking a preliminary step to the side or by changing the weight to the opposite foot on beats 4 1

GUAPACHA TIMING ("Guapacha" is pronounced "Whappacha") (L&F)

This interesting variation of timing lends itself to certain figures and may be used for examinations and medal tests (Silver upwards). It is described below on a Left Foot Time Step
Commence with feet apart, weight on RF

	Count	Beat Value
Hold position with weight on RF	2	3/4
LF behind RF, toe slightly turned out (Ball of foot)	a	1/4
Replace weight to RF	3	1
LF to side to chasse LRL	4&1	1/2. 1/2. 1

Other syllabus figures suited to Guapacha timing are the New York to LSP and RSP, Cross Basic and 6 - 10 of Fan (development)

FORWARD WALKS (A,L&F)

1   Commence, for example, with RF forward, LF held back with pressure on inside edge of toe. (Both legs straight)

2   Using the "settling" hip movement commence to move body weight forward

3   Move LF forward with knee slightly flexed, first on toe, then on ball of foot. Lower heel and straighten leg just before the extent of the stride. Release right heel

4   With a smooth action take weight over LF. Allow RF to turn out, completing the rotational hip movement

5   Retain tone in right leg with pressure on inside edge of toe. (Both legs are now straight)

Continue with a RF Walk in the same manner

Note   Because of the turnout of the RF the toe will end in line with heel of LF

When a Forward Walk is followed by a weight transference back the following differences occur

1   The toe of front foot is turned out

2   The body is not committed to continue to move forward after the step is placed

3   The back knee will flex and veer towards the front knee causing no turn out of back foot. End with pressure on ball of back foot (Example Man's step 1 of Closed Basic Movement)

BACKWARD WALKS (A,L&F)

1   Commence, for example, with LF back, RF held forward with heel released and pressure on toe. (Both legs straight)

2   Using the "settling" hip movement commence to move RF back on ball of foot, knee slightly flexed, until it passes under the body, then extend back to toe

3   With a smooth action take weight over RF. Straighten right knee and lower right heel. A natural turn out of RF occurs, completing the "rotational" hip action

4   During the weight change release left heel without bending the knee, allowing a slight straightening of LF

5   Retain tone in left leg, with pressure on left toe. (Both legs are now straight)

        Continue with a LF Walk in the same manner

Note   Because of the turnout of the RF the toe will end in line with heel of LF

PRESSED FORWARD WALK (A,L&F)

1   Place foot forward on ball of foot with part weight, small step Knee flexed

2   Take full weight on to foot, lowering heel and straightening knee during the last half beat of music
        (Example Step 5 of Lady's Closed Hip Twist)

PRESSED BACKWARD WALK (A,L&F)

1   Place foot back on ball of foot with part weight. Knee flexed

2   Take full weight on to foot, lowering heel and straightening knee during the last half beat of music
        (Example Cuban Cross position as step 1 of Man's Natural Top)

EXTENDED FORWARD WALK (A,L&F)

1   Point foot forward with slight pressure on outside edge of toe. Knee straight

2   Take weight on to foot, lowering heel during the last half beat of music
        (Example Step 6 of Lady's Alemana when alternative method is used)

THE CHA CHA CHA CHASSE AND ALTERNATIVES

The 4th beat in each bar of music is divided into two equal parts, each part using a half beat. The first two steps of the Cha Cha Cha Chasse are taken on these two half beats (counts '4 and') and the third step is taken on the first beat of the following bar of music, (count '1')

In its basic form this chasse is a group of three steps taken in any forward, backward or sideways direction, with the second step moving towards (or to) the other foot
Steps 1 and 2 have equal weight distribution (Exception Twist Chasse)

The chasse may also be danced in place or with or without turn

In the charts, for simplicity, only the foot position of the first step of each chasse is given (Example RF forward to chasse RLR). Where the third step of the chasse differs the position is given. The type of chasse used is also given (Examples Forward Lock, Compact Chasse etc)

Detailed descriptions of the various chasses listed will be required in the examination room

(St,A,L&F)	Chasse to Side (Man or Lady)	Count
1	LF to side, small step. Knee commences to straighten	4
2	Move RF towards LF (or close RF to LF) Knee slightly relaxed	and
3	LF to side. Knees straight, hips to left	1
Footwork	Ball flat on each step	

A Chasse to right side would be the normal opposite, starting with RF

(St,A,L&F)	Compact Chasse	Count
1	Close LF to RF. left knee commences to straighten	4
2	Transfer weight to RF. right knee commences to straighten	and
3	Transfer weight to LF. Knee straight, hips to left	1
Footwork	Ball flat on each step	

Another alternative to the Compact Chasse danced on 3 - 5 of Alemana and Hockey Stick Man may dance a small step to side LF, transfer weight to RF, and close LF to RF (Count '4 and 1')

THE CHA CHA CHASSE (continued)

(St,A,L&F) **Right Foot Forward Lock (Man or Lady)**		**Count**
1	RF forward small step. Right knee straight	4
2	LF behind RF (Cuban Cross) Hips central	and
3	RF forward, having moved it slightly rightwards Knees straight	1

Footwork　　1 Ball flat　　2 Toe　　3 Ball flat

A Left Foot Forward Lock would be the normal opposite, starting with LF

(St,A,L&F) **Left Foot Backward Lock (Man or Lady)**		**Count**
1	LF back small step, toe turned out. Left Knee slightly flexed	4
2	RF in front of LF (Cuban Cross)	and
3	LF back, having moved it slightly leftwards. Knees straight	1

Footwork　　1 Toe　　2 Ball flat　　3 Ball flat

A Right Foot Backward Lock would be the normal opposite starting with RF

If preferred a simple forward or backward chasse may be used in place of the Forward and Backward Lock for the lower grade tests.
(Social Dance, Pre-Bronze and Bronze)

Split Cuban Break Chasse (Man or Lady) (St,A,L&F)

1	RF fwd and across toe turned out small step R knee straight, L knee slightly flexed
2	Replace weight to LF
3	RF side R knee straight, hip to R

FORWARD OR BACKWARD RUNS

These are three small steps forward or back and are part of the There and Back **(St,A,L&F)** and Sweetheart **(F)**

Backward Runs may be used in place of 3 - 5 of Open Basic Movement and Forward Runs in place of 8 - 10 (Lady normal opposite) All levels

(L&F) Forward Runs may be used in place of the Forward Lock danced on 8 - 10 of Hockey Stick or Spiral when ended in Left Side Position, or in place of the Forward Lock in The Chase

Footwork Ball flat on each step

Knee commences to straighten on each step

CHA CHA CHA CHASSE (continued)

(L&F)	Ronde Chasse (Man or Lady)	Count
1	Circle LF outwards with toe in contact with floor towards end of preceding beat of music, then place LF behind RF (Cuban Cross) Hips central	4
2	RF fwd and slightly to side, small step. Right knee commences to straighten, hips slightly to right	and
3	LF to side. Knees straight, hips to left	1
Footwork	1-3 Ball flat (Late lowering of heel on 1)	
(L)	Man may dance a Ronde Chasse in place of 3 - 5 of Alemana or Hockey Stick, closing LF to RF on last step	
(F)	Man dances a Ronde Chasse on 3 - 5 of Hip Twist Spiral and he may also use it in place of 3 - 5 of Advanced Hip Twist The Ronde Chasse may be danced by Man and Lady in place of 3 - 5 of Man's Basic Movement when in Right Side, Right Shadow or Tandem Position, using same foot as partner	

(L&F)	Twist Chasse (Man or Lady)	Count
1	RF forward, Pressed Forward Walk, having turned 1/4 to left towards end of preceding beat of music	4
2	Turn 1/4 to right on RF and close LF to RF. Knees relaxed, hips central	and
3	RF to side. Knees straight, hips to right	1
Footwork	1 Ball 2 Balls of both feet 3 Ball flat	
Note	Turn on 1 is initiated from the hips, which are turned more than the upper body	
(L)	Man may dance a Twist Chasse in place of the last three steps of any figure ended in Fan Position	
(F)	Lady dances a Twist Chasse on 3 - 5 of Hip Twist Spiral, and she may also use it in place of steps 3 - 5 of Advanced Hip Twist It may be danced by Man and Lady in place of 8 - 10 of Man's Basic Movement when in Right Side, Right Shadow or Tandem Position, using the same foot as partner	

CHA CHA CHA CHASSE (continued)

(L&F)	Slip Chasse (Man)	Count
1	LF back, part weight, toe turned out, Hips rotate slightly to left	4
2	Draw RF back about 8cm (3 inches). Right knee slightly flexed	and
3	Close LF to RF slightly forward. Left knee straight, hips to left	1
Footwork	1 Inside edge of toe 2 Flat 3 Ball flat	

Man dances the Slip Chasse on 3 - 5 of Open Hip Twist; he may also use it in place of 3 - 5 of Alemana, Hockey Stick or Closed Hip Twist **(F)** Turkish Towel or Sweetheart

(F)   **RUNAWAY CHASSE (LADY)**

Commence with LF crossed in front of RF having danced a Spiral Turn to left (7/8 turn) on step 7 of preceding figure

		Count
1	LF fwd, small step. Turn 1/8 left. Left knee straight, hips neutral	4
2	RF fwd (Pressed FWD Walk), hips to left	and
3	Turn 1/2 to right to end LF back and slightly to side in Fan or Open Position. Both knees straight, hips to left	1
Footwork	1-3 Ball flat (Late lowering of heel on 2)	

(F)   Lady may dance the Runaway Chasse in place of steps 8 - 10 of Fan (development), Spiral, Curl and Open or Advanced Hip Twist

TURN OUT OF FOOT

There is a natural turn out of the foot on backward and side steps. The amount of turn out will be approximately 1/16th to 1/8th depending on the dancer's own physique. This turn out also occurs on a forward step when the forward movement is checked and followed by a weight change to the back foot. (Example Step 1 of Closed Basic Movement). On other forward steps the tracking of the moving foot is straighter, and as the weight is taken on to the front foot the back foot is allowed to turn out naturally

FOOT POSITIONS

These refer to the position of one foot in relation to the other when the foot has arrived in position; for example, forward, back side, etc. Fan Position, Open Position, etc., are also given in the Foot Position column for clarity

It must be understood that when moving the foot from one position to another the leg must always track "under" the body

All forward open turns will be commenced as a forward step passing under the body and ending to side, back, back and slightly to side etc. (example Step 6 Closed Basic Movement as Man)

All backward open turns will be commenced as a backward step passing under the body ending to side, side and slightly back etc (Example Step 3 Closed Basic Movement as Man)

The amount of turn generally dictates the degree of travel forward or back made by the working foot after it has passed the supporting foot

Explanations of some other terms used in the Foot Position column are as follows

TRANSFER OR REPLACE

The word "transfer" denotes a step which has remained with pressure on the floor at the end of the preceding step. (Example Steps 2 and 7 of the Closed Basic Movement). The word "replace" denotes a step where pressure is released from the floor at the end of the preceding step. (Example The feet are replaced when dancing Basic Movement in Place)

CUBAN CROSS (A,L&F)

This term denotes a position where, for example, the RF is behind LF, right toe opposite or just past left heel, toe turned out. (Example Man's step 1 of Natural Top). The exact distance between the toe of the back foot and heel of the front foot will depend on the dancer's own physique or the figure danced. This also applies when the LF is behind RF in the same position, and when the RF or LF is in front, heel opposite or just past the toe, with toe turned out

STUDY ALIGNMENT

Study alignments are given in the Cha Cha Cha to facilitate ease of learning. It is unnecessary to adhere to these suggested alignments and they will not be asked in the examination room

On side steps and closing steps the terms "facing" or "backing" are used, referring to the position of the body in relation to the room

Direction is given on forward or backwards steps. This refers to the direction in which the step is taken in relation to the room. Terms used, for example, are "down LOD", "against LOD", "diagonally to centre", "diagonally to wall" etc

Occasionally the term "pointing" is used, this refers to the alignment of the foot to illustrate certain positions where the body has turned less than the foot. (Example Man's step 3 of Advanced Hip Twist)

When a precise alignment is not given it denotes there may be a permissible variation in the amount of turn used

ALIGNMENT IN RELATION TO ROOM

AMOUNT OF TURN

This is generally measured from the alignment or direction of one step to the alignment or direction of the next and is given as a guide; more or less turn can often be made when dancing the figures

NOTE **A turn made on the supporting foot before the next step is placed will be commenced towards the end of the preceding beat and is normally counted "and" or "a" for teaching purposes**

When a precise amount of turn is not given over two steps it denotes there can be acceptable deviations to allow for individual speed or turn and expression; for example the amount of turn for the Natural Top in the Cha Cha Cha is up to three complete turns over steps 1-15.

AMOUNTS OF TURN
(This diagram represents one complete turn)

FOOTWORK

This refers briefly to the parts of the foot used when taking a step. The footwork on most steps is ball flat. There will be a little more pressure towards the inside edge of the ball of foot as it moves into position. As this is the footwork on most steps in Cha Cha Cha only the exceptions are given in the charts to facilitate ease of learning. Part of the foot is in contact with the floor at all times

The footwork of the Chasses and Alternatives is described under this heading. For simplicity this will not be repeated in the charts

Points to Remember

1.   On forward steps the heel of front foot will lower just before the extent of the stride

2.   As weight is taken on to a forward or side step the heel of the non - supporting foot will be released with inside edge of ball of foot in contact with floor

3.   As weight is taken on to a backward step using a full beat of music the heel of front foot is slightly released from floor

4.   When a turn is made on the supporting foot prior to the placing of next step the footwork will be ball flat, then turn is made on ball of foot keeping foot flat

SPECIAL NOTE CONCERNING THE LADY'S TURN ON STEPS 7 AND 8 OF SOME FIGURES ENDED IN OPEN OR FAN POSITION

Because of slight deviations of speed of body turn the Lady's turn may be more gradual; she may prefer to turn 3/8 to left between 6 and 7 to end with RF back and slightly to side, making a further 1/8 between 7 and 8. This deviation is acceptable in both theory and demonstration

Figures concerned are

Fan (Development) - Hockey Stick - Closed Hip Twist - Open Hip Twist - Spiral - Curl - Advanced Hip Twist - Hockey Stick ending to Turkish Towel

LEADS

Leads may be loosely divided into four categories as follows

1	**Weight changes**	Lady will follow Man's change of weight
2	**Physical**	Man conveys the lead by increasing the tone in his arm(s) resulting in pressure felt through the hands. Lady responds with matching tone and will continue to move in the direction indicated, until the Man's hand restricts her movement, then she will turn to a different direction
3	**Shaping**	Man conveys the position required by "shaping" his body and arms. For example, on 6-10 of Alemana Lady accepts the direction of movement indicated by Man's left hand. Man must ensure Lady's right hand is over her own right shoulder, above head level, so that her balance remains undisturbed; he will circle his hand in a clockwise direction when turning Lady to right and in an anti-clockwise direction when turning her left
4	**Visual**	When dancing without hold Lady may copy the man's steps
		The Leads are given in the charts as a guide but have not been explained in great detail thus allowing individual interpretation

PRECEDES AND FOLLOWS

The listed Precedes and Follows given for each figure are all that are necessary for the theoretical section of the professional examination; these are clearly classified for Student - Teacher, Association, Licentiate and Fellow

The Student - Teacher will be required to know one Precede and Follow to each figure, the Associate two, and the Licentiate and Fellow three (where applicable)

1 CLOSED BASIC MOVEMENT (St,A,L&F)

Commence in Closed Position

MAN	Foot Position	Amount of Turn	Lead	Count
1	LF fwd		Weight change	2
2	Transfer weight to RF		,,	3
3-5	LF to side and slightly back to chasse LRL	1/8 to L over 2 - 5	,,	4&1
6	RF back		,,	2
7	Transfer weight to LF		,,	3
8-10	RF to side to chasse RLR	1/8 to L over 7 - 10	,,	4&1

Study Alignment 1 To Wall   2 To centre   3 - 5 End backing DC against LOD   6 DC against LOD   7 DW   8 - 10 End facing LOD

LADY	Foot Position	Amount of Turn	Count
1	RF back		2
2	Transfer weight to LF		3
3-5	RF to side to chasse RLR	1/8 to L over 2 - 5	4&1
6	LF fwd		2
7	Transfer weight to RF		3
8-10	LF to side and slightly back to chasse LRL	1/8 to L over 7 - 10	4&1

Study Alignment 1 To wall   2 To centre   3 - 5 End facing DC against LOD   6 DC against LOD   7 DW   8 - 10 End backing LOD

CLOSED BASIC MOVEMENT (continued)

Notes

1   Amount of Turn   Up to 1/4 turn L may be made over 2 -5 and 7 - 10. Beginners and "below Bronze" medal candidates may find it easier to make no turn on the Closed Basic Movement, in which case both Man and Lady will dance a side Chasse on 3 - 5 and 8 - 10

2   Hold   Although Closed Position is retained throughout the arm connection must allow for a slight alteration of body alignment and distance in relation to partner

3   The Closed Basic Movement may end with Man and Lady turning to Open CPP over 8 - 10, Man turning 1/8 R and Lady 1/8 L, Man release R hand hold

Precedes   **(St)**   Closed or Open Basic Movement - New York to RSP ended facing partner - Spot or Switch Turn to L (Lady to R) - Underarm Turn to R - R Side Shoulder to Shoulder ended facing partner - Hand to Hand to LSP - Three Cha Cha Chas Fwd in Closed Position - Side Step to L or R commenced with RF - There and Back - RF Time Step

(A)   Three Cha Cha Chas Fwd in LSP ended facing partner - Alemana

(L&F)   Reverse Top - Rope Spinning - Cross Basic - RF Cuban Break - Split Cuban Break commenced with LF

Into steps 6 - 10

(St)   1 - 5 Open Basic Movement - New York to LSP ended facing partner - Spot or Switch Turn to R (Lady to L) - Underarm Turn to L - L Side Shoulder to Shoulder ended facing partner - Hand to Hand to RSP - Three Cha Cha Chas Back - Side Step to L or R commenced with LF - LF Time Step

(A)   Three Cha Cha Chas Fwd in RSP ended facing partner - Natural Opening Out Movement

(L&F)   1 - 5 Cross Basic - LF Cuban Break - Split Cuban Break commenced with RF

CLOSED BASIC MOVEMENT (continued)

Follows	**(St)**	Closed or Open Basic Movement - New York to LSP having turned to Open CPP over 8 - 10 - Spot or Switch Turn to R (Lady to L) - Underarm Turn to L - L Side Shoulder to Shoulder - Side Step to L or R commenced with LF - Hand to Hand to RSP with alternative hold - There and Back - LF Time Step
	(A)	Fan
	(L&F)	Cross Basic - LF Cuban Break - Split Cuban Break commenced with LF

From steps 1.2

(St,A,L&F) Three Cha Cha Chas Back

From steps 1 - 5

	(St)	6 - 10 Open Basic Movement - Spot or Switch Turn to L (Lady to R) - Underarm Turn to R - Hand to Hand to LSP - Side Step to L or R commenced with RF
	(A,L&F)	Natural Top (3 - 5 LF side to chasse, turning slightly R. Lady Chasse fwd)

From steps 1 - 7

(St,A,L&F) Three Cha Cha Chas Fwd

Development

	(L&F)	Turn 3/8 to L over 7 - 10 to Contact Position, Man taking the Chasse to side and slightly fwd (Lady 8 - 10 LF behind RF, as Cuban Cross, to Chasse LRL)
		Follow with 6 - 10 or 6 - 15 of Reverse Top

BASIC MOVEMENT IN PLACE (St,A,L&F)

This is a figure where five steps are danced in place with feet almost together, LF RF LF RF LF (LF Basic in Place) or RF LF RF LF RF (RF Basic in Place). Lady dances normal opposite. It is danced in Closed Position and there is no turn. This is a useful practice exercise for teaching beginners the weight changes and rhythm and may also be used as an occasional alternative to the normal Closed Basic Movement. It is not listed separately in the Precedes and Follows

OPEN BASIC MOVEMENT (St,A,L&F)

This figure is similar to the Closed Basic Movement danced without turn, except that the first Chasse is danced back and the second Chasse forward. (Lady normal opposite). It may be danced in Closed or (A,L&F) Open Position

This figure may be danced with normal hold, L to R hand hold, or without hold. All levels

Precedes		When danced in Closed Position
	(St,A,L&F)	As for Closed Basic Movement
		When danced in Open Position
	(A)	Three Cha Cha Chas Fwd in Open Position - Hockey Stick - Closed Hip Twist ended in Open Position
	(L)	Open Hip Twist, Spiral or Curl ended in Open Position - Chase
	(F)	Advanced Hip Twist ended in Open Position - Turkish Towel - Follow my Leader
Follows		When danced in Closed Position
	(St,A,L&F)	Closed or Open Basic Movement
From steps 1.2		Three Cha Cha Chas Back
From steps 1 - 5		6 - 10 Closed Basic Movement - Natural Top (Man taking the chasse to side, turning slightly to R)
From steps 1 - 7		Three Cha Cha Chas Fwd
Follows		When danced in Open Position
	(A)	Open Basic Movement - Alemana
	(L)	Open Hip Twist - Curl - Chase
	(F)	Turkish Towel - Sweetheart - Follow my Leader
From steps 1.2	**(A,L&F)**	Three Cha Cha Chas Back
From steps 1 - 5	**(A,L&F)**	Natural Top (Man taking the chasse to side, turning slightly to R)
From steps 1 - 7	**(A,L&F)**	Three Cha Cha Chas Fwd

2 NEW YORK TO LEFT SIDE POSITION (St,A,L&F)

Commence in Open CPP. L to R hand hold

MAN	Foot Position	Amount of Turn	Lead	Count
1	LF fwd in LSP	1/8 to R	Increase tone in L arm and turn it with body over 1 - 5	2
2	Transfer weight to RF			3
3-5	LF to side to chasse LRL End in Open PP	3/8 to L over 3 - 5	Take required hold at end of 5	4&1

Study Alignment   Commence facing DW against LOD   1 Against LOD
2 Down LOD   3 - 5 End facing DW

On step 1 turn is made towards end of previous beat of music

LADY	Foot Position	Amount of Turn	Count
1	RF fwd in LSP	1/8 to L	2
2	Transfer weight to LF		3
3-5	RF to side to chasse RLR End in Open PP	3/8 to R over 3 - 5	4&1

Study Alignment   Commence facing DC against LOD   1 Against LOD
2 Down LOD   3 - 5 End facing DC

On step 1 turn is commenced towards end of previous beat of music

Precedes   All ended in Open CPP

(St)   Closed Basic Movement - New York to RSP -
Spot or Switch Turn to L (Lady to R) -
Underarm Turn to R - Hand to Hand to LSP
- Three Cha Cha Chas Fwd in LSP - Side Step to
R commenced with RF

(A)   R Side Shoulder to Shoulder with L to R hand
hold - Alemana - Hockey Stick - Closed Hip
Twist

(L)   Open Hip Twist - Curl - Spiral - Rope Spinning -
Cross Basic - RF Cuban Break - Split Cuban
Break commenced with LF

(F)   Advanced Hip Twist - Hip Twist Spiral

Follows   When ended in Open PP

(St & A)   New York to RSP - Spot or Switch Turn to L
(Lady to R)

(L&F)   RF Cuban Break - Split Cuban Break commenced with RF

Follows   When ended facing partner (1/4 turn over 3 - 5)

(St)   6 - 10 Closed or Open Basic Movement -
Underarm Turn to R - Hand to Hand to LSP -
Side Step to R commenced with RF - RF Time
Step

(A)   6 - 10 Fan - 6 - 10 Closed Hip Twist

(L&F)   RF Cuban Break - Split Cuban Break commenced with RF

Notes   **(A,L&F)**   RSP may be achieved by turning 1/8 more
between 5 of New York and 1 of next figure, to
follow with 4 - 9 Three Cha Cha Chas Fwd

The New York may also be danced from Three
Cha Cha Chas Fwd in LSP. (No turn on 1 of
New York)

NEW YORK TO RIGHT SIDE POSITION (St,A,L&F)

Commence in Open PP. R to L hand hold

MAN	Foot Position	Amount of Turn	Lead	Count
1	RF fwd in RSP	1/8 to L	Increase tone in R arm and turn it with body over 1 - 5	2
2	Transfer weight to LF			3
3-5	RF to side to chasse RLR End in Open CPP	3/8 to R over 3 - 5	Take required hold at end of 5	4&1

Study Alignment   Commence facing DW   1 Down LOD   2 Against LOD
3 - 5 End facing DW against LOD

On step 1 turn is commenced towards end of previous beat of music

LADY	Foot Position	Amount of Turn	Count
1	LF fwd in RSP	1/8 to R	2
2	Transfer weight to RF		3
3-5	LF to side to chasse LRL End in Open CPP	3/8 to L over 3 - 5	4&1

Study Alignment   Commence facing DC   1 Down LOD   2 Against LOD
3 - 5 End facing DC against LOD

On step 1 turn is commenced towards end of previous beat of music

Precedes		All ended in Open PP
	(St)	New York to LSP - Spot or Switch Turn to R (Lady to L) - Underarm Turn to L - Hand to Hand to RSP - Three Cha Cha Chas Fwd in RSP - Side Step to L commenced with LF (L to R hand hold)
	(A)	L Side Shoulder to Shoulder (L to R hand hold)
	(L&F)	LF Cuban Break - Split Cuban Break commenced with RF
Follows		When ended in Open CPP
	(St & A)	New York to LSP - Spot or Switch Turn to R (Lady to L) - Underarm Turn to L
	(L&F)	LF Cuban Break - Split Cuban Break commenced with LF
Follows		When ended facing partner (1/4 turn over 3 - 5)
	(St)	Closed or Open Basic Movement - Hand to Hand to RSP - Side Step to R or L commenced with LF - There and Back - LF Time Step
	(A)	Fan
	(L&F)	Cross Basic - LF Cuban Break - Split Cuban Break commenced with LF
Notes	**(A,L&F)**	LSP may be achieved by turning 1/8 more between 5 of New York and 1 of the next figure, to follow with 4 - 9 Three Cha Cha Chas Fwd
		The New York may also be danced from Three Cha Cha Chas Fwd in RSP. (No turn on 1 of New York)

27

3   SPOT TURNS (including Switch Turns and Underarm Turns) (St,A,L&F)

Spot Turns are two forward steps and a Chasse to side danced solo by Man and/or Lady, circling either to L or R. When turning to L commence with RF. When turning to R commence with LF. If preferred when turning L the ball of LF may remain in place while the turn is made around the foot. Likewise the ball of RF may remain in place when turning R

When danced at the same time as partner, Man turns L and Lady turns R, or vice versa. Spot Turns may also be danced individually by Man or Lady while partner dances, for example, a Time Step or 5 steps of Closed Basic Movement. The Spot Turn is a popular ending to New York, Hand to Hand and many other figures, and may also be danced as a Switch Turn as described in the following charts

A complete turn is made when couple commence and end facing each other 7/8 turn is made when commenced in Open PP or Open CPP and ended facing partner, or when commenced facing partner and ended in Open PP or Open CPP
3/4 turn is made when commenced in Open PP and ended in Open CPP or vice versa, or when commenced in R or LSP and ended facing partner

The commencing and finishing hold will depend on the preceding and following figure. These are listed at the end of the Switch Turn charts

Development (L&F)   The Spot or Switch Turn to L (Lady to R) may be ended in Open Position, taking L to R hand hold at end of 2, and taking the Chasse forward leading Lady back

SWITCH TURN TO LEFT (St,A,L&F)

Commence in Closed Position, No hold, or L to R or R to L hand hold

MAN	Foot Position	Amount of Turn	Lead	Count
1	RF fwd in line with LF, then turn to end RF back	1/4 to L, then a further 1/2	When commenced with one hand hold increase tone in arm and turn it with body, then release hold	2
2	Transfer weight to LF			3
3-5	RF to side to chasse RLR	1/4 to L over 3-5	Take required hold at end of 5	4&1

Study Alignment Commence facing wall 1 Down LOD. End backing LOD 2 Against LOD   3 - 5 End facing wall

On step 1 turn is commenced towards end of previous beat of music

LADY	Foot Position	Amount of Turn	Count
1	LF fwd in line with RF, then turn to end LF back	1/4 to R, then a further 1/2	2
2	Transfer weight to RF		3
3-5	LF side to chasse LRL	1/4 to R over 3 - 5	4&1

Study Alignment   Commence facing centre   1 Down LOD. End backing LOD   2 Against LOD   3 - 5 End facing centre

On step 1 turn is commenced towards end of previous beat of music

Precedes	**(St)**	1 - 5 Closed Basic Movement - New York to LSP - Spot or Switch Turn to R (Lady to L) - L Side Shoulder to Shoulder ended facing partner - Hand to Hand to RSP - Side Step to L commenced with LF - LF Time Step
	(A)	Three Cha Cha Chas Fwd in RSP - L Side Shoulder to Shoulder with one hand hold ended in Open PP
	(L&F)	LF Cuban Break - Split Cuban Break commenced with RF
Follows	**(St)**	Closed or Open Basic Movement - New York to LSP - Spot or Switch Turn to R (Lady to L) - Underarm Turn to L - Hand to Hand to RSP - Side Step to L or R commenced with LF - There and Back
	(A)	4 - 9 Three Cha Cha Chas Fwd in LSP - Fan
	(L&F)	Cross Basic - LF Cuban Break - Split Cuban Break commenced with LF
Follows		When ended in Open Position
	(L)	Open Basic Movement - 1.2 Open Basic Movement into Three Cha Cha Chas Back or 1 - 5 Open Basic Movement into Natural Top - Alemana - Open Hip Twist - Curl - Chase
	(F)	Turkish Towel - Sweetheart - Follow My Leader

Note For alternative starting and finishing positions see Spot turns page 28

SWITCH TURN TO RIGHT (St,A,L&F)

Commence in Closed Position. No hold, or L to R or R to L hand hold

MAN	Foot Position	Amount of Turn	Lead	Count
1	LF fwd in line with RF, then turn to end LF back	1/4 to R, then a further 1/2	When commenced with one hand hold increase tone in arm and turn it with body, then release hold	2
2	Transfer weight to RF			3
3-5	LF to side to chasse LRL	1/4 to R over 3-5	Take required hold at end of 5	4&1

Study Alignment   Commence facing wall   1 Against LOD. End backing against LOD   2 Down LOD   3 - 5 End facing wall

On step 1 turn is commenced towards end of previous beat of music

LADY	Foot Position	Amount of Turn	Count
1	RF fwd in line with LF, then turn to end RF back	1/4 to L, then a further 1/2	2
2	Transfer weight to LF		3
3-5	RF side to chasse RLR	1/4 to L over 3 - 5	4&1

Study Alignment   Commence facing centre   1 Against LOD. End backing against LOD   2 Down LOD   3 - 5 End facing centre

On step 1 turn is commenced towards end of previous beat of music

Precedes	**(St)**	Closed Basic Movement - New York to RSP - Spot or Switch Turn to L (Lady to R) - Underarm Turn to R - R Side Shoulder to Shoulder ended facing partner - Hand to Hand to LSP - There and Back - Side Step to R commenced with RF - RF Time Step
	(A)	Three Cha Cha Chas Fwd in LSP - Alemana, Hockey Stick, Closed Hip Twist or R Side Shoulder to Shoulder with L to R hand hold (all ended in open CPP)
	(L)	Open Hip Twist, Spiral, Curl, Rope Spinning or Cross Basic (all ended in Open CPP) - RF Cuban Break - Split Cuban Break commenced with LF
	(F)	Advanced Hip Twist ended in Open CPP - Closed or Open Hip Twist Spiral
Follows	**(St)**	6 - 10 Closed or Open Basic Movement - New York to RSP - Spot or Switch Turn to L (Lady to R) - Underarm Turn to R - Hand to Hand to LSP - Side Step to L or R commenced with RF - RF Time Step
	(A)	4 - 9 Three Cha Cha Chas Fwd in RSP - 6 - 10 Fan
	(L&F)	Aida - RF Cuban Break - Split Cuban Break commence with RF
Note		For alternative starting and finishing positions see Spot Turns page 28

UNDERARM TURN TO LEFT (St,A,L&F)

May be commenced in Closed Position or Open CPP. L to R hand hold

From Closed Position

Man dances 1 - 5 of Closed Basic Movement, while leading Lady to dance a Spot or Switch Turn to L underarm by raising L arm and circling it in anti-clockwise direction

From Open CPP

Man dances 1 - 5 of Closed Basic Movement taking the first step towards Lady's L side and turning 1/8 L over 3 - 5. Lead as above

Man may turn 1/8 L on last step to end in Open PP (Lady turns 1/8 less)

Precedes	**(St&A)**	Closed Basic Movement - New York to RSP - Spot or Switch Turn to L (Lady to R) - Underarm Turn to R - R Side Shoulder to Shoulder - Hand to Hand to LSP - Side Step to R commenced with RF - RF Time Step
		Three Cha Cha Chas Fwd in LSP ended facing partner or in Open CPP - R Side Shoulder to Shoulder (L to R hand hold) ended in Open CPP
	(L&F)	RF Cuban Break - Split Cuban Break commenced with LF
Follows	**(St)**	6 - 10 Closed or Open Basic Movement - New York to RSP - Spot or Switch Turn to L (Lady to R) - Underarm Turn to R - Hand to Hand to LSP - Side Step to L or R commenced with RF - RF Time Step
	(A)	6 - 10 Fan - Natural Top (turning slightly R on preceding Chasse)
	(L&F)	Aida - RF Cuban Break - Split Cuban Break commenced with RF

UNDERARM TURN TO RIGHT (St,A,L&F)

Commence in Closed Position. L to R hand hold

Man dances 6 - 10 of Closed Basic Movement (no turn) while leading Lady to dance a Spot or Switch Turn to R underarm by raising L arm and circling it in a clockwise direction.

Man may turn 1/8 R on last step to end in Open CPP (Lady turn 1/8 less)

Precedes   **(St&A)**   1 - 5 Closed Basic Movement - New York to LSP ended facing partner - Spot or Switch Turn to R (Lady to L) - Underarm Turn to L - L Side Shoulder to Shoulder ended facing partner - Hand to Hand to RSP
Three Cha Cha Chas Fwd in RSP - Side Step to L or R commenced with LF

         (L&F)   1 - 5 Cross Basic - LF Cuban Break - Split Cuban Break commenced with RF

Follows   **(St)**   Closed or Open Basic Movement - New York to LSP - Spot or Switch Turn to R (Lady to L) - Underarm Turn to L - L Side Shoulder to Shoulder - Hand to Hand to RSP - Side Step to L or R commenced with LF - There and Back - LF Time Step - 4 - 9 Three Cha Cha Chas Fwd in LSP

         (A)   Fan
         (L&F)   LF Cuban Break - Split Cuban Break commenced with LF

NOTES

35

4 LEFT SIDE SHOULDER TO SHOULDER (St,A,L&F)

Commence in Closed Position

MAN	Foot Position	Amount of Turn	Lead	Count
1	LF fwd towards Lady's L side	No turn	Weight change	2
2	Transfer weight to RF		"	3
3-5	LF to side to chasse LRL End LF side and slightly fwd	1/4 to L over 3 - 5	"	4&1

Study Alignment   1 DW against LOD   2 DC   3 - 5 End facing DW

LADY	Foot Position	Amount of Turn	Count
1	RF back	No turn	2
2	Transfer weight to LF towards Man's L side		3
3-5	RF to side to chasse RLR End RF side and slightly back	1/4 to L over 3 - 5	4&1

Study Alignment   1 DW against LOD   2 DC   3 - 5 End backing DW

LEFT SIDE SHOULDER TO SHOULDER (continued)

Precedes   Last step of preceding figure RF side and slightly fwd. (Lady LF side and slightly back) Hold may be released

(St,A,L&F) Closed Basic Movement turning 1/8 R on last step - Underarm Turn to R (Man turning 1/8 R on last step. Lady 1.1/8 R) - R Side Shoulder to Shoulder - Side Step to R commenced with RF (1/8 R on 5)

(A,L&F) Alemana (Man turning 1/8 to R on last step)

Follows   **(St,A,L&F)** R Side Shoulder to Shoulder

Follows   When ended facing partner, having turned 1/8 over 3 - 5 and danced the Chasse to side

(St) 6 - 10 Closed or Open Basic Movement - Spot or Switch Turn to L (Lady to R) - Underarm Turn to R - Hand to Hand to LSP - Side Step to L or R commenced with RF - RF Time Step

(A) 6 - 10 Fan, Closed Hip Twist or Alamana

(L&F) RF Cuban Break - Split Cuban Break commenced with RF

Development (A,L&F) Following the Hockey Stick the Shoulder to Shoulder may be danced with L to R, no hold or "double" hand hold, commencing with the L Side Shoulder to Shoulder. Man keeps the L hand higher than usual to prevent Lady moving too far back on steps 8 - 10 of the Hockey Stick, although the couple will be further apart than when dancing the figure in Closed Position. When danced this way it may be ended on Open PP. (Lady no turn)

Follows   When ended in Open PP

(A) Spot or Switch Turn to L (Lady to R) - New York to RSP - 4 - 9 Three Cha Cha Chas Fwd in RSP

(L&F) RF Cuban Break - Split Cuban Break commenced with RF

Example amalgamation Hockey Stick (moving towards Lady's L side over steps 8 - 10), L Side Shoulder to Shoulder, R Side Shoulder to Shoulder, L Side Shoulder to Shoulder ended in Open PP, Spot or Switch Turn to L (Lady to R)

RIGHT SIDE SHOULDER TO SHOULDER (St,A,L&F)

Commence in Closed Position

MAN	Foot Position	Amount of Turn	Lead	Count
1	RF fwd towards Lady's R side	No turn	Weight change	2
2	Transfer weight to LF		"	3
3-5	RF to side to chasse RLR End RF side and slightly fwd	1/4 to R over 3 - 5	"	4&1

Study Alignment   1 DW   2 DC against LOD   3 - 5 End facing DW
against LOD

LADY	Foot Position	Amount of Turn	Count
1	LF back	No turn	2
2	Transfer weight to RF towards Man's R side		3
3-5	LF to side to chasse LRL End LF side and slightly back	1/4 to R over 3 - 5	4&1

Study Alignment   1 DW   2 DC against LOD   3 - 5 End backing DW
against LOD

RIGHT SIDE SHOULDER TO SHOULDER (continued)

Precedes   Last step of preceding figure LF side and slightly fwd. (Lady RF side and slightly back) Hold may be released

        (St,A,L&F) L Side Shoulder to Shoulder - Side Step to L commenced with LF (1/8 L on 3, Man side and slightly fwd, Lady side and slightly back)

Follows   **(St,A,L&F)** L Side Shoulder to Shoulder

Follows   When ended facing partner, having turned 1/8 over 3 - 5 and danced the Chasse to side

        (St)   Closed or Open Basic Movement - Spot or Switch Turn to R (Lady to L) - Underarm Turn to L - Hand to Hand to RSP - Side Step to L or R commenced with LF - There and Back - LF Time Step

        (A)   Fan

        (L&F)   LF Cuban Break - Split Cuban Break commenced with LF

Development **(A,L&F)**   The R Side Shoulder to Shoulder may be danced with L to R or "double" hand hold following a L Side Shoulder to Shoulder danced in this manner. When these holds are used it may be ended in Open CPP (Lady no turn)

Follows   When ended in Open CPP

        (A)   New York to LSP - Spot or Switch Turn to R - (Lady to L) - Underarm Turn to L - 4 - 9 Three Cha Cha Chas
Fwd in LSP

        (L&F)   LF Cuban Break - Split Cuban Break commenced with LF

5 HAND TO HAND TO RIGHT SIDE POSITION (St,A,L&F)

Commence in Closed Position. R to L hand hold

MAN	Foot Position	Amount of Turn	Lead	Count
1	LF back in RSP	1/4 to L	Increase tone in R arm and turn it with body over 1 - 5	2
2	Transfer weight to RF			3
3-5	LF to side to chasse LRL	1/4 to R over 3 - 5	Take required hold at end of 5	4&1

Study Alignment Commence facing wall 1 Against LOD 2 Down LOD 3 - 5 End facing wall

On step 1 turn is commenced towards end of previous beat of music

LADY	Foot Position	Amount of Turn	Count
1	RF back in RSP	1/4 to R	2
2	Transfer weight to LF		3
3-5	RF to side to chasse RLR	1/4 to L over 3 - 5	4&1

Study Alignment Commence facing centre 1 Against LOD 2 Down LOD 3 - 5 End facing centre

On step 1 turn is commenced towards end of previous beat of music

Notes Man and Lady

1   Man take R to L hand hold at end of previous figure, simultaneously releasing L to R hand hold where necessary

2   The Hand to Hand to RSP may be ended in Open PP. (1/8 over 3 - 5)

Precedes   **(St)**   Closed Basic Movement - New York to RSP ended facing partner - Spot or Switch Turn to L (Lady to R) - Underarm Turn to R - R Side Shoulder to Shoulder ended facing partner - Hand to Hand to LSP - There and Back - Side Step to R commenced with RF - RF Time Step

(A)   Three Cha Cha Chas Fwd in LSP ended facing partner - Alemana (both dancing the second chasse to side)

(L&F)   Rope Spinning (both dancing the second chasse to side) - RF Cuban Break - Split Cuban Break commenced with LF

Follows   **(St)**   6 - 10 Closed or Open Basic Movement - New York to RSP - Spot or Switch Turn to L (Lady to R) - Underarm Turn to R - Hand to Hand to LSP - Side Step to L or R commenced with RF - RF Time Step

(A)   6 - 10 Fan (Lady in line on 6) - 6 - 10 Closed Hip Twist (leading Lady with R hand to turn R then changing to L to R hand hold on 7)

(L&F)   Aida - Spiral ending (Man almost closes LF to RF on 3 to chasse and leads Lady into her spiral action on 5 to continue with 6 - 10 of Spiral) - RF Cuban Break - Split Cuban Break commenced with RF

Follow from step 2

(St,A,L&F) Three Cha Cha Chas Fwd in RSP

Alternative Hold

(St,A,L&F) The figure may be commenced with normal hold, Man allowing R hand to slide little further around Lady's back on 1, releasing hold with L hand. Lady slide L hand naturally across Man's shoulder. When following with Hand to Hand to LSP Man places L hand on Lady's back releasing R hand hold at end of 5, while Lady rests R hand lightly across Man's L shoulder. Man's hand on Lady's back is just below her shoulder blade

HAND TO HAND TO LEFT SIDE POSITION (St,A,L&F)

Commence in Closed Position. L to R hand hold

MAN	Foot Position	Amount of Turn	Lead	Count
1	RF back in LSP	1/4 to R	Increase tone in L arm and turn it with body over 1 - 5	2
2	Transfer weight to LF			3
3-5	RF to side to chasse RLR	1/4 to L over 3 - 5	Take required hold at end of 5	4&1

Study Alignment   Commence facing wall   1 Down LOD   2 Against LOD
3 - 5 End facing wall

On step 1 turn is commenced towards end of previous beat of music

LADY	Foot Position	Amount of Turn	Count
1	LF back in LSP	1/4 to L	2
2	Transfer weight to RF		3
3-5	LF to side to chasse LRL	1/4 to R over 3 - 5	4&1

Study Alignment   Commence facing centre   1 Down LOD   2 Against
LOD   3 - 5 End facing centre

On step 1 turn is commenced towards end of previous beat of music

Notes Man and Lady

1   Man take L to R hand hold at end of previous figure, simultaneously releasing R to L hand hold where necessary

2   The Hand to Hand to LSP may be ended in Open CPP. (1/8 over 3 - 5)

HAND TO HAND TO LEFT SIDE POSITION (continued)

Precedes   **(St)**   1 - 5 Closed Basic Movement - New York to LSP ended facing partner - Spot or Switch Turn to R (Lady to L) - Underarm Turn to L - L Side Shoulder to Shoulder ended facing partner - Hand to Hand to RSP - Side Step to L commenced with LF - LF Time Step

          (A)   Three Cha Cha Cha Fwd in RSP ended facing partner

          (L&F)   LF Cuban Break - Split Cuban Break commenced with RF

Follows   **(St)**   Closed or Open Basic Movement - New York to LSP - Spot or Switch Turn to R (Lady to L) - Underarm Turn to L - Hand to Hand to RSP - Side Step to L or R commenced with LF - There and Back - LF Time Step

          (A)   Fan

          (L&F)   Rope Spinning (Man almost close RF to LF on 3 to chasse, leading Lady into her spiral action on 5 to continue with Rope Spinning) - LF Cuban Break - Split Cuban Break commenced with LF

Follow from step 2

          (St,A,L&F)   Three Cha Cha Chas Fwd in LSP

Alternative Hold   Please refer to Alternative Hold for Hand to Hand to RSP on page 41

6   THREE CHA CHA CHAS (St,A,L&F)

(St,A,L&F) Three Forward Locks may be danced progressively in one direction counted '4 and 1, 2 and 3, 4 and 1'. The following methods may be used:-
In Closed Position with normal hold, L to R hand hold, low double hand hold alternating "Contra" Hand Hold (Pat a Cake) no hold

(A,L&F) In Open Position (Holds as above)

Method 1		**THREE CHA CHA CHAS BACK**

Man three Backward Locks commenced with LF (Lady three Forward Locks commenced with RF)

Precedes   **(St,A,L&F)** 1.2 Closed or Open Basic Movement

Follows   **(St)**   6 - 10 Closed or Open Basic Movement - 6.7 Closed or Open Basic Movement into Three Cha Cha Chas Fwd

(A,L&F)   6 - 10 Fan - 6 - 10 Alemana Natural Top (Man last step LF side turning slightly R. Lady RF fwd)

Method 2   **THREE CHA CHA CHAS FORWARD**

Man three Forward Locks commenced with RF (Lady three Backward Locks commenced with LF)

Precedes   **(St)**   1 - 7 Closed or Open Basic Movement
(A,L&F)   1 - 7 Hockey Stick

Follows   **(St)**   Closed or Open Basic Movement
(A)   Fan - Alemana
(L)   Open Hip Twist, Curl or Chase (when Three Cha Cha Chas are danced in Open Position)
(F)   Turkish Towel, Sweetheart or Follow My Leader (when Three Cha Chas are danced in Open Position)

THREE CHA CHA CHAS (continued)

Method 3

THREE CHA CHA CHAS FORWARD IN RIGHT SIDE POSITION

Man and Lady dance three Forward Locks, Man commencing LF, Lady RF (A slight turn to R, L and R may be made alternately on each Lock. Lady normal opposite)

Precedes   (St,A,L&F) 1.2 Hand to Hand to RSP

Precedes to steps 4 - 9   (all ended in Open PP)

    (St)   New York to LSP - Spot or Switch Turn to R (Lady to L) - Underarm Turn to L

    (A,L&F)   L Side Shoulder to Shoulder

Follows   (St,A,L&F) New York from RSP - Spot or Switch Turn to L (Lady to R)

Note   The last three steps may be danced as a Side Chasse, Man and Lady turning to face partner to end in Closed Position. Follows as from 1-5 Closed Basic Movement

Method 4

THREE CHA CHA CHAS FORWARD IN LEFT SIDE POSITION

Man and Lady dance three Forward Locks, Man commencing RF Lady LF (A slight turn to L, R and L may be made alternately on each Lock. Lady normal opposite)

Precedes   (St,A,L&F) 1.2 Hand to Hand to LSP

Precedes to steps 4 - 9   (all ended in Open CPP)

    (St)   New York to RSP - Spot or Switch Turn to L (Lady to R) - Underarm Turn to R

    (A)   R Side Shoulder to Shoulder - Alemana - Hockey Stick - Closed Hip Twist

    (L)   Open Hip Twist - Spiral - Curl - Rope Spinning

    (F)   Advanced Hip Twist - Hip Twist Spiral

Follows   (St,A,L&F) New York from LSP - Spot or Switch Turn to R (Lady to L)

Note   The last three steps may be danced as a Side Chasse, Man and Lady turning to face partner to end in Closed Position. Follows as from Closed Basic Movement

45

7 SIDE STEP TO LEFT (Commenced with LF) (St,A,L&F)

Commence in Closed Position

MAN	Foot Position	Amount of Turn	Lead	Count
1	LF to side	No turn	Weight change	2
2	Close RF to LF	,,	,,	3
3-5	LF to side to chasse LRL	,,	,,	4&1

Study Alignment   Facing wall

LADY	Foot Position	Amount of Turn	Count
1	RF to side	No turn	2
2	Close LF to RF	,,	3
3	RF to side to chasse RLR	,,	4&1

Study Alignment   Facing centre

Notes Man and Lady

1   When the preceding figure ends with feet apart the Man will brush LF to RF towards end of count '1'. (Lady brush RF to LF)

2   L to R hand hold may be used

3   When L to R hand hold is used 5 may be turned to end in Open PP (Man 1/8 L, Lady 1/8 R)

4   The Side Step may be curved to L or R

Precedes   **(St)**   Closed Basic Movement - New York to RSP ended facing partner - Spot or Switch Turn to L (Lady to R) - Underarm Turn to R - R Side Shoulder to Shoulder ended facing partner - Hand to Hand to LSP - Side Step to L commenced with RF - RF Time Step

 (A)   Alemana (ended to side) - Three Cha Cha Chas Fwd in LSP ended facing partner

 (L&F)   Rope Spinning (ended to side) - RF Cuban Break - Split Cuban Break commenced with LF

Follows   **(St&A)**   6 - 10 Closed or Open Basic Movement - New York to RSP - Spot or Switch Turn to L (Lady to R) - Underarm Turn to R - R Side Shoulder to Shoulder (1/8 turn L on 5) - Hand to Hand to LSP - Side Step to L commenced with RF - RF Time Step

 (L&F)   RF Cuban Break - Split Cuban Break commenced with RF

SIDE STEP TO LEFT (Commenced with RF) (St,A,L&F)

Commence in Closed Position

MAN	Foot Position	Amount of Turn	Lead	Count
1	Close RF to LF	No turn	Weight change	2
2	LF to side	,,	,,	3
3	Move RF towards LF (or close)	,,	,,	4
4	LF to side	,,	,,	&
5	Move RF towards LF (or close)	,,	,,	1

Study Alignment   Facing wall

LADY	Foot Position	Amount of Turn	Count
1	Close LF to RF	No turn	2
2	RF to side	,,	3
3	Move LF towards RF (or Close)	,,	4
4	RF to side	,,	&
5	Move LF towards RF (or close)	,,	1

Study Alignment   Facing centre

Notes Man and Lady
1   L to R hand hold may be used
2   The Side Step may be curved to L or R

Precedes	**(St)**	1 - 5 Closed Basic Movement - New York to LSP ended facing partner - Spot or Switch Turn to R (Lady to L) - Underarm Turn to L - L Side Shoulder to Shoulder ended facing partner - Hand to Hand to RSP - Side Step to L commenced with LF - LF Time Step
	(A)	Three Cha Cha Chas Fwd in RSP ended facing partner
	(L&F)	LF Cuban Break - Split Cuban Break commenced with RF
Follows	**(St)**	Closed or Open Basic Movement - There and Back - Side Step to L commenced with LF
	(A,L&F)	Fan

47

SIDE STEP TO RIGHT (Commenced with LF) (St,A,L&F)

Commence in Closed Position

MAN	Foot Position	Amount of Turn	Lead	Count
1	Close LF to RF	No turn	Weight change	2
2	RF to side	,,	,,	3
3	Move LF towards RF (or close)	,,	,,	4
4	RF to side	,,	,,	&
5	Move LF towards RF (or close)	,,	,,	1

Study Alignment   Facing centre

LADY	Foot Position	Amount of Turn	Count
1	Close RF to LF	No turn	2
2	LF to side	,,	3
3	Move RF towards LF (or Close)	,,	4
4	LF to side	,,	&
5	Move RF towards LF (or close)	,,	1

Study Alignment   Facing wall

Notes Man and Lady
1   L to R hand hold may be used
2   The Side Step may be curved to R or L

Precedes	(St)	Closed Basic Movement - New York to RSP ended facing partner - Spot or Switch Turn to L (Lady to R) - Underarm Turn to R - R Side Shoulder to Shoulder ended facing partner - Hand to Hand to LSP - Side Step to R commenced with RF - RF Time Step
	(A)	Alemana (ended to side) - Three Cha Cha Chas Fwd in LSP ended facing partner
	(L&F)	Rope Spinning (ended to side) RF Cuban Break - Split Cuban Break commenced with LF
Follows	(St)	6 - 10 Closed or Open Basic Movement - Underarm Turn to R - Side Step to R commenced with RF
	(A,L&F)	6 - 10 Fan

48

SIDE STEP TO RIGHT (Commenced with RF) (St,A,L&F)

Commence in Closed Position

MAN	Foot Position	Amount of Turn	Lead	Count
1	RF to side	No turn	Weight change	2
2	Close LF to RF	,,	,,	3
3-5	RF to side to chasse RLR	,,	,,	4&1

Study Alignment   Facing centre

LADY	Foot Position	Amount of Turn	Count
1	LF to side	No turn	2
2	Close RF to LF	,,	3
3	LF to side to chasse LRL	,,	4&1

Study Alignment   Facing wall

Notes Man and Lady

1   When the preceding figure ends with feet apart the Man will brush RF to LF towards end of count '1'. (Lady brush LF to RF)

2   L to R hand hold may be used

3   5 may be turned to end in Open CPP (Man 1/8 R, Lady 1/8 L)

4   The Side Step may be curved to L or R

Precedes	**(St)**	1 - 5 Closed Basic Movement - New York to LSP ended facing partner - Spot or Switch Turn to R (Lady to L) - Underarm Turn to L - L Side Shoulder to Shoulder ended facing partner - Hand to Hand to RSP - Side Step to R commenced with LF - LF Time Step
	(A)	Three Cha Cha Chas Fwd in RSP ended facing partner
	(L&F)	LF Cuban Break - Split Cuban Break commenced with RF
Follows	**(St)**	Closed or Open Basic Movement - New York to LSP - Spot or Switch Turn to R (Lady to L) - L Side Shoulder to Shoulder (1/8 turn R on 5) - Hand to Hand to RSP - Side Step to R commenced with LF - LF Time Step
	(A)	Fan
	(L&F)	LF Cuban Break - Split Cuban Break commenced with LF

8 THERE AND BACK (St,A,L&F)

Commence in Closed Position

MAN	Foot Position	Amount of Turn	Lead	Count
1	Close LF to RF	No turn	Weight change	2
2	Replace weight to RF	”	”	3
3-5	Three small steps back LRL (Backward Runs)	”	Increase tone in arms moving them slightly fwd on 3, then release hold. 4&5 visual	4&1
6	RF back	”	Visual	2
7	Transfer weight to LF	”	”	3
8-10	Three small steps fwd RLR (Forward Runs) End in Closed Position	”	Visual Take required hold on 10	4&1

Study Alignment   1.2 Facing wall   3 - 6 To centre   7 - 10 To wall

THERE AND BACK (continued)

LADY	Foot Position	Amount of Turn	Count
1	Close RF to LF	No turn	2
2	Replace weight to LF	,,	3
3-5	Three small steps back RLR (Backward Runs)	,,	4&1
6	LF back	,,	2
7	Transfer weight to RF	,,	3
8-10	Three small steps fwd LRL (Forward Runs)	,,	4&1

Study Alignment   1.2 Facing centre   3 - 6 To Wall   7 - 10 To centre

Precedes	**(St)**	Closed or Open Basic Movement - New York to RSP ended facing partner - Spot or Switch Turn to L (Lady to R) - Underarm Turn to R - R Side Shoulder to Shoulder ended facing partner - Hand to Hand to LSP - Three Cha Cha Chas Fwd in Closed Position - Side Step to L or R commenced with RF - There and Back - RF Time Step
	(A)	Three Cha Cha Chas fwd in LSP ended facing partner - Alemana
	(L&F)	Reverse Top - Rope Spinning - Cross Basic - RF Cuban Break - Split Cuban Break commenced with LF
Follows	**(St)**	Closed or Open Basic Movement - Spot or Switch Turn to R (Lady to L) - Underarm Turn to L - Side Step to L or R commenced with LF - Hand to Hand to RSP - There and Back - LF Time Step
	(A)	Fan
	(L&F)	LF Cuban Break - Split Cuban Break commenced with LF

9 TIME STEPS (St,A,L&F)

Time Steps may be danced at any time when in Closed or Open Position without hold, or having released hold at end of the preceding figure. They may be commenced with either foot, Man dancing a LF Time Step while Lady dances a RF Time Step, or vice versa

Alternatively Man may dance a Spot or Switch Turn or **(L&F)** a Cuban Break, while Lady dances a Time Step, or vice versa

LEFT FOOT TIME STEP (Man and Lady)

Commence in Closed Position, without hold or **(L&F)** Open Position

MAN LADY	Foot Position	Amount of Turn	Lead	Count
1	LF behind RF (Cuban Cross)	No turn	Visual	2
2	Replace weight to RF	,,	,,	3
3	LF to side to chasse LRL	,,	,,	4&1

Study Alignment   Facing wall or centre

Note	**(L&F)**	When Guapacha timing is used (see page 7) the heel will not be lowered in step 1
Precedes	**(St)**	Closed Basic Movement - New York to RSP (ended facing partner) - Spot or Switch Turn to L (Lady to R) - Underarm Turn to R - R Side Shoulder to Shoulder (ended facing partner) - Hand to Hand to LSP - Side Step to R commenced with RF - RF Time Step
	(A)	Alemana - Hockey Stick - Closed Hip Twist (ended in Open Position)
	(L)	Open Hip Twist, Spiral or Curl (ended in Open Position) - Cross Basic - RF Cuban Break - Split Cuban Break commenced with LF - Chase
	(F)	Advanced Hip Twist (ended in Open Position) - Turkish Towel - Follow My Leader
Follows	**(St&A)**	6 - 10 Closed or Open Basic Movement - New York to RSP - Spot or Switch Turn to L (Lady to R) - Underarm Turn to R - R Side Shoulder to Shoulder - Hand to Hand to LSP - Side Step to L or R commenced with RF - RF Time Step
	(L&F)	RF Cuban Break - Split Cuban Break commenced with RF

TIME STEPS (continued)

RIGHT FOOT TIME STEP (Man and Lady)

Commence in Closed Position, without hold or **(L&F)** Open Position

MAN LADY	Foot Position	Amount of Turn	Lead	Count
1	RF behind LF (Cuban Cross)	No turn	Visual	2
2	Replace weight to LF	,,	,,	3
3	RF to side to chasse RLR	,,	,,	4&1

Study Alignment   Facing wall or centre

Because there is no physical lead the following type of amalgamation is often used:-
Man and Lady dance two Time Steps (Man commencing LF, Lady RF)
Man dances a Spot or Switch Turn to R or **(L&F)** a LF Cuban Break (Lady RF Time Step)
Man dances a RF time step while Lady 'accepts the challenge' and dances a Spot or Switch Turn to R or **(L&F)** a LF Cuban Break

Note	**(L&F)**	When Guapacha timing is used (see page 7) the heel will not be lowered in step 1
Precedes	**(St&A)**	1 - 5 Closed Basic Movement - New York to LSP (ended facing partner) - Spot or Switch Turn to R (Lady to L) - Underarm Turn to L - L Side Shoulder to Shoulder (ended facing partner) - Hand to Hand to RSP - Side Step to L commenced with LF - LF Time Step
	(L&F)	LF Cuban Break - Split Cuban Break commenced with RF
Follows	**(St)**	Closed or Open Basic Movement - New York to LSP - Spot or Switch Turn to R (Lady to L) - Underarm Turn to L - L Side Shoulder to Shoulder - Hand to Hand to RSP - Side Step to L or R commenced with LF - LF Time Step
	(A)	Fan - Alemana (from Open Position)
	(L)	Open Hip Twist - Curl - Cross Basic - LF Cuban Break - Split Cuban Break commenced with LF - Chase
	(F)	Turkish Towel - Sweetheart - Follow My Leader

53

10   FAN (A,L&F)

Commence in Closed Position

MAN	Foot Position	Amount of Turn	Lead	Count
1	LF fwd		Weight changes	2
2	Transfer weight to RF	1/8 to L over 2 - 5	”	3
3-5	LF to side and slightly back to chasse LRL		”	4&1
6	RF back	No turn	Lower L arm to L side at waist level	2
7	Transfer weight to LF	”	Increase tone in L arm. Release R hand hold	3
8-10	RF to side to chasse RLR End in Fan Position	”	Slightly extend L arm. L hand still	4&1

Study Alignment   1 DW against LOD   2 - 5 Turn over 2 - 5 to end backing centre   6 To centre   7 To wall   8 - 10 Facing wall

LADY	Foot Position	Amount of Turn	Count
1	RF back		2
2	Transfer weight to LF	1/8 to L over 2 - 5	3
3-5	RF to side to chasse RLR		4&1
6	LF fwd		2
7	RF back and slightly to side	1/8 to L	3
8-10	Bwd Lock LRL End in Fan Position	1/8 to L	4&1

Study Alignment   1 DW against LOD   2 - 5 Turn over 2 - 5 to end facing centre   6 To centre   7 DW   8 - 10 Backing LOD

FAN (continued)

Precedes   **(A)**   Closed or Open Basic Movement - New York to RSP ended facing partner - Spot or Switch Turn to L (Lady to R) - Underarm Turn to R - R Side Shoulder to Shoulder ended facing partner - Hand to Hand to LSP - Three Cha Cha Chas Fwd (or in LSP ended facing partner) - Side Step to L or R commenced with RF - There and Back - RF Time Step - Alemana - Natural Top

            (L&F)   Reverse Top - Rope Spinning - Cross Basic - RF Cuban Break - Split Cuban Break commenced with LF

Into steps 6 - 10 (A)   New York to LSP ended facing partner - Spot or Switch Turn to R (Lady to L) - Underarm Turn to L - L Side Shoulder to Shoulder ended facing partner - Hand to Hand to RSP - Three Cha Cha Chas Back in Closed Position - Side Step to L commenced with LF - Side Step to R commenced with LF - Natural Opening Out Movement

            (L&F)   1 - 5 Cross Basic - LF Cuban Break - Split Cuban Break commenced with RF

Follows   **(A,L&F)**   Alemana - Hockey Stick

Alternative amount of turn   Man may make 1/4 turn L over steps 2 - 5 and 1/8 over 7 - 10 (Lady 1/4 L over 2 - 5 and 3/8 over 7 - 10)

FAN Development (L&F)

Commence in Closed Position

MAN	Foot Position	Amount of Turn	Lead	Count
1	LF fwd		Weight change	2
2	Transfer weight to RF	1/4 to L over 2 - 5	,,	3
3-5	LF to side to chasse LRL End in PP		Lower L arm to a Promenade shape	4&1
6	RF back		L arm to L side	2
7	Transfer weight to LF	1/8 to L over 7 - 10	Increase tone in L arm. Release R hand hold	3
8-10	RF to side to chasse RLR End in Fan Position		Slightly extend L arm. L hand still	4&1

Study Alignment 1 DW against LOD   2 - 5 Turn over 2 - 5 to end facing DW   6 DC against LOD   7 - 10 Turn over 7 - 10 to end facing LOD

FAN Development (L&F) (continued)

LADY	Foot Position	Amount of Turn	Count
1	RF back	No turn	2
2	Transfer weight to LF	,,	3
3-5	Diag Fwd Lock RLR End in PP	,,	4&1
6	LF fwd passing in front of Man's body	1/8 to L	2
7	RF fwd in line with LF, then turn to end RF back	1/2 to L Body turns less	3
8-10	Bwd Lock LRL End in Fan Position	Body completes turn	4&1

Study Alignment   1 DW against LOD   2 DC   3 - 5 DC   6 To centre
7 To centre. End backing centre   8 - 10 To centre

Amount of Turn   See SPECIAL NOTE on page 17

Note   **(F)**   Man and Lady. Guapacha timing could be used on 6 - 10

11   ALEMANA (A,L&F)

Commence in Fan Position

MAN	Foot Position	Amount of Turn	Lead	Count
1	LF fwd	No turn	Slightly release L arm tone	2
2	Transfer weight to RF	,,	Contract L arm	3
3-5	Compact Chasse LRL	,,	Gradually raise L hand above Lady's R shoulder	4&1
6	RF back	,,	Circle L hand clockwise over 6 - 9	2
7	Transfer weight to LF	,,		3
8-10	Compact Chasse RLR End in Closed Position	,,	Lower L arm to required hold at end of 10	4&1

Study Alignment   1 To wall   2 To centre   3 - 5 Backing centre
6 To centre   7 To wall   8 - 10 Facing wall

LADY	Foot Position	Amount of Turn	Count
1	Close RF to LF	No turn	2
2	LF fwd	,,	3
3-5	Fwd Lock RLR	1/8 to R between 4 & 5	4&1
6-10	Two fwd steps and a Fwd Lock under raised arms L R LRL End in Closed Position	1.1/8 to R over 6 - 10	2.3 4&1

Study Alignment   1 Backing LOD   2 Against LOD   3 - 5 Against LOD.
End R toe pointing DC against LOD   6 - 10 Turn over 6 - 10 to end to centre

Alternative Method   Lady may use an Extended Forward Walk on 6

ALEMANA (continued)

Precedes	(A)	Fan - Closed Hip Twist
	(L)	Open Hip Twist - Opening Out from Reverse Top - Spiral - Curl - Cross Basic ended in Fan Position
	(F)	Advanced Hip Twist - Sweetheart

The Alemana may be commenced in Open Position

(Lady steps back on 1 instead of closing RF to LF, and makes a complete turn R over 6 - 10)

Precedes   All ended in Open Position

	(A)	Open Basic Movement - Three Cha Cha Chas Fwd - RF Time Step - Hockey Stick - Closed Hip Twist
	(L)	Spot or Switch Turn to L (Lady to R) - Open Hip Twist - Spiral or Curl - Chase
	(F)	Advanced Hip Twist - Turkish Towel - Follow My Leader

Follows	(A,L&F)	Closed or Open Basic Movement - There and Back - Fan

Alternative Finishing Positions and their Follows

1   **Man and Lady end to side**

	(A)	Hand to Hand to RSP - Side Step to L commenced with LF - Side Step to R commenced with LF - LF Time Step
	(L&F)	Cross Basic

2   **Man and Lady end diagonally fwd in Open CPP**

(Man 1/8 to R on 8 arresting Lady's turn with L hand. Lady 1.1/8 R over 5 - 8)

	(A)	New York from LSP - Spot or Switch Turn to R (Lady to L) - Underarm Turn to L - 4 - 9 Three Cha Cha Chas Fwd in LSP
	(L&F)	LF Cuban Break - Split Cuban Break commenced with LF

3   **Lady end fwd towards Man's R side**

(Man turns body slightly R on 8 to lead Lady towards his R side. Lady LF fwd in line with RF into FWD Lock)
Man LF slightly leftwards on 7

(A)   Natural Opening Out Movement - Closed Hip Twist

(L&F)   Spiral - Rope Spinning

4   **Man and Lady fwd towards partner's R side**

(Man RF fwd in line with LF on 8, into Fwd Lock towards Lady's R side. Lead, placement of LF on 7 and Lady's steps as position 3. Man may make up to 1/4 R over 8 - 10, adjusting Lady's turn accordingly)

(F)   Advanced Hip Twist - Hip Twist Spiral

Development **(F)** The Alemana may be danced with R to R hand hold. Precede with Hockey Stick or any figure ended in Open Position, Man changing Lady's R hand into his R hand on the last step and releasing hold with L hand. Lady makes a complete turn R on the Alemana, Man taking 8 fwd in line with LF towards partner's R side into Fwd Lock. Lead, placement of LF on 7 and Lady's steps as position 3. Follow with the Advanced Hip Twist, Man changing Lady's R hand into his L hand, releasing hold with R hand on 7

12   HOCKEY STICK (A,L&F)

Commence in Fan Position

MAN	Foot Position	Amount of Turn	Lead	Count
1	LF fwd	No turn	Slightly release L arm tone	2
2	Transfer weight to RF	"	Contract L arm	3
3-5	Compact Chasse LRL	"	Gradually raise L hand in front of Lady's head	4&1
6	RF behind LF (Cuban Cross)	1/8 to R	Extend L arm over 6 & 7	2
7	LF fwd small step	No turn	Lower L arm to waist level at end of 7	3
8-10	Fwd Lock in Open Position RLR	"	Slightly extend L arm fwd	4&1

Study Alignment   1 To wall   2 To centre   3 - 5 Backing centre   6 DC
7 - 10 DW against LOD

62

HOCKEY STICK (continued)

LADY	Foot Position	Amount of Turn	Count
1	Close RF to LF	No turn	2
2	LF fwd	"	3
3-5	Fwd Lock RLR	"	4&1
6	LF fwd	1/8 to L	2
7	RF fwd in line with LF, then turn underarm to end RF back	1/2 to L Body turns less	3
8-10	Bwd Lock in Open Position LRL	Body completes turn	4&1

Study Alignment   1 Backing LOD   2 - 5 Against LOD   6 Against LOD to end DW against LOD   7 DW against LOD. End backing DW against LOD 8 - 10 DW against LOD

Amount of Turn   See SPECIAL NOTE on page 17

63

HOCKEY STICK (continued)

Precedes	(A)	Fan - Closed Hip Twist
	(L)	Open Hip Twist - Opening Out from Reverse Top - Spiral - Curl - Cross Basic ended in Fan Position
	(F)	Advanced Hip Twist - Sweetheart

Into step 6 - 10

	(L&F)	1- 10 Natural Top
Follows	(A)	Open Basic Movement - L Side Shoulder to Shoulder - 1.2 Open Basic Movement into Three Cha Cha Chas Back or 1 - 5 Open Basic Movement into Natural Top - LF Time Step - Alemana
	(L)	Open Hip Twist - Curl - Chase
	(F)	Turkish Towel - Sweetheart - Follow My Leader

From steps 1 - 7

	(A,L&F)	Three Cha Cha Chas Fwd in Open Position

Alternative Finishing Positions and their Follows

1   **Open CPP**

Man leads Lady to overturn towards end of 7, both taking 8 diagonally fwd in Open CPP to chasse. (Lady turns an additional 1/4 L on RF using a loosely crossed spiral action)

The Associate is not required to explain the spiral action and it is not necessarily expected below Gold Medallist level in tests

(A,L&F)	New York to LSP - Spot or Switch Turn to R (Lady to L) - Underarm Turn to L - 4 - 9 Three Cha Cha Chas Fwd in LSP

2   **Left Side Position**

Man leads Lady to overturn towards end of 7, then turns 1/8 R to chasse fwd, lowering L arm and taking it fwd to below shoulder level. (Lady turns towards end of 7 as for CPP above, then turns an additional 1/8 L, to chasse fwd). Forward Runs could be used in place of last chasse

(L&F)	Spot or Switch Turn to R (Lady to L) - New York to LSP (no turn on first step) - 4 - 9 Three Cha Cha Chas Fwd in LSP - LF Cuban Break (Lady RF) retaining LSP, or Split Cuban Break commenced with LF (Lady RF)

NOTES

13   NATURAL TOP (A,L&F)

Commence in Closed Position

MAN	Foot Position	Amount of Turn	Lead	Count
1	RF behind LF (Cuban Cross)	Up to three complete turns over 1 - 15	Weight change	2
2	LF to side		"	3
3-14	Repeat 1 & 2 six times		"	4&1 2.3 4&1 2.3 4&
15	Close RF to LF		"	1

Study Alignment   Commence facing wall. End facing wall when maximum turn is used

Footwork   Heel of RF need not lower fully on 1,3,5,7,9,11 & 13 and should never lower until the LF commences to move for the next step

Note   Steps 1, 7 & 11 are Pressed Backward Walks

LADY	Foot Position	Amount of Turn	Count
1	LF to side	Up to three complete turns over 1 - 15	2
2	RF in front of LF toe turned out		3
3-14	Repeat 1 & 2 six times		4&1 2.3 4&1 2.3 4&
15	LF to side		1

Study Alignment   Commence facing centre. End facing centre when maximum turn is used

NATURAL TOP (continued)

Precedes	**(A,L&F)**	1 - 5 Closed or Open Basic Movement or Underarm turn to L, Man taking the chasse to side turning slightly to R (Lady Fwd Lock) - Three Cha Cha Chas Back (Man end last chasse LF side turning slightly R)
Follows	**(A)**	Closed or Open Basic Movement - Fan - Natural Opening Out Movement* - Closed Hip Twist*
	(L)	Spiral* - Rope Spinning*
		* On the last step of Natural Top Man leads Lady towards his R side
	(F)	Man RF fwd in line with LF on 13 into Fwd Lock RLR (Lady Fwd Lock towards Man's R side) continuing to turn up to 1/4 R to follow with Advanced Hip Twist or Hip Twist Spiral (Alternative RF fwd in line with LF on 15, Lady LF fwd towards Man's R side)
From step 10	**(L&F)**	6 - 10 Hockey Stick

Notes

1		The couple will circle around an imaginary spot centred between them, keeping the bodies centred to each other
2		Because of the continuous turn knees will not straighten fully, therefore only a slight, natural hip movement is used
3		Five steps of Natural Top may be danced, namely 11 - 15
Development	**(F)**	While continuing to dance 6.7 of Natural Top lead Lady to turn L under raised L arm having released R hand hold (Lady RF fwd and slightly across LF, turning 1/4 L on 6, then continue to turn L on RF and LF side almost facing partner on 7). Regain normal hold and continue with 8 - 15 of Natural Top (Lady's turn between 6 & 7 will depend on Man's turn)

14 NATURAL OPENING OUT MOVEMENT (A,L&F)

Commence in Closed Position

MAN	Foot Position	Amount of Turn	Lead	Count
1	LF to side or fwd in RSP	Slight body turn to R	Increase tone and lower L arm to R at chest level. Widen R arm in hold to R side	2
2	Transfer weight to RF		Retain tone in arms	3
3-5	Compact Chasse LRL End in Closed Position	Slight body turn to L to normal positions over 3 - 5	Gradually return arms to required hold	4&1

Study Alignment 1 - 5 Facing wall

LADY	Foot Position	Amount of Turn	Count
1	RF back in RSP	1/2 to R	2
2	Transfer weight to LF		3
3-5	RF fwd and slightly across LF to chasse RLR, to end RF to side in Closed Position	1/4 to L then a further 1/4 over 4 & 5	4&1

Study Alignment 1 To centre 2 To wall 3 - 5 Down LOD. End facing centre

On step 1 turn is commenced towards end of previous beat of music

NATURAL OPENING OUT MOVEMENT (continued)

Precedes   **(A)**   Natural Top - Alemana
            (L&F) Rope Spinning

(On Alemana **(A)** and Rope Spinning **(L&F)** Man turns body slightly R on 8 to lead Lady towards his R side. Lady LF fwd in line with RF to Fwd Lock LRL, Man LF slightly leftwards on 7)

Follows   **(A)**   6 - 10 Closed or Open Basic Movement - Underarm Turn to R - 6 - 10 Fan
            (L&F) Reverse Top (Man turns 1/8 L over 3 - 5 to Contact Position, placing LF in front of RF as Cuban Cross to chasse LRL. Lady turns an additional 1/8 over 3 - 5 to end with RF back and slightly side. Man's first step of Natural Opening Out Movement is side)

15   CLOSED HIP TWIST (A,L&F)

Commence in Closed Position

MAN	Foot Position	Amount of Turn	Lead	Count
1	LF to side or fwd in RSP	Slight body turn to R	Increase tone and lower L arm to R at chest level. Widen R arm in hold to R side	2
2	Transfer weight to RF		Retain tone in arms	3
3-5	Compact Chasse LRL	Very slight body turn to L	Retain tone and return arms to normal position, slightly to R	4&1
6	RF back	Slight body turn to L to normal position	Towards end of preceding beat lower L arm to a Promenade shape, then L arm to L side	2
7	Transfer weight to LF	No turn	Increase tone in L arm. Release R hand hold	3
8-10	RF to side to chasse RLR End in Fan Position	"	Slightly extend L arm. L hand still	4&1

Study Alignment   1 - 5 Facing wall   6 To centre   7 To wall
8 - 10 Facing wall

CLOSED HIP TWIST (continued)

LADY	Foot Position	Amount of Turn	Count
1	RF back in RSP	1/2 to R	2
2	Transfer weight to LF		3
3-5	RF fwd in line with LF towards Man's R side to chasse RLR	1/2 to L	4&1
6	LF fwd passing in front of Man	1/4 to R	2
7	RF fwd in line with LF, then turn to end RF back	1/2 to L Body turns less	3
8-10	Bwd Lock LRL End in Fan Position	Body completes turn	4&1

Study Alignment   1 To centre   2 To wall   3 - 5 To centre   6 Down LOD
(RF pointing DW)   7 Down LOD. End backing LOD   8 - 10 Down LOD

Amount of Turn   See SPECIAL NOTE on page 17

On steps 1, 3 and 6 turn is commenced towards end of previous beat of music

Notes   **1**   Step 3 is similar to a Pressed Forward Walk but the heel is not lowered and the knee remains flexed

   2   Step 5 is a Pressed Forward Walk

   3   Turn on 6 is initiated from the hips, which are turned more than the upper body

CLOSED HIP TWIST (continued)

Precedes	**(A)**	Natural Top - Alemana
	(L&F)	Rope Spinning

Note   On Alemana **(A)** and Rope Spinning **(L&F)** Man turns body slightly R on 8 to lead Lady towards his R side. (Lady LF fwd in line with RF to chasse LRL) Man LF slightly leftwards on 7

Into steps 6 - 10 (A&L)   Hand to Hand to RSP (Lead Lady to turn R with R to L hand hold on 6. Change to L to R hand hold on 7) Left side Shoulder to Shoulder ended facing partner

Follows   **(A,L&F)**   Alemana - Hockey Stick

Alternative Finishing Positions and their Follows

1   **Open Position**
(Man turns 1/4 to L over 7 - 10)

(A)	Open Basic Movement - 1.2 Open Basic Movement into Three Cha Cha Chas Back or 1 - 5 Open Basic Movement into Natural Top - LF Time Step - Alemana
(L)	Open Hip Twist - Curl - LF Cuban Break - Split Cuban Break commenced with LF - Chasse
(F)	Turkish Towel - Sweetheart - Follow My Leader

2   **Open CPP**
(Man turn 1/8 L over 7 & 8 leading Lady to overturn on 7, both taking 8 diagonally fwd to chasse in Open CPP. Lady turns an additional 1/8 L on 7 using a loosely crossed spiral action)
The Associate is not required to explain the spiral action and it is not necessarily expected below Gold medallist level in tests

(A)	New York to LSP - Spot or Switch Turn to R (Lady to L) - Underarm Turn to L - 4 - 9 Three Cha Cha Chas Fwd in LSP
(L&F)	LF Cuban Break - Split Cuban Break commenced with LF

3   **Contact Position**
(Man 1/2 L over 7 - 10 dancing the chasse side and slightly fwd. Lady 3/4 L over 7 - 10 dancing the chasse with LF behind RF as Cuban Cross. Normal hold retained throughout)

(L&F)	6 - 10 or 6 - 15 Reverse Top

16 OPEN HIP TWIST (L&F)

Commence in Open Position

MAN	Foot Position	Amount of Turn	Lead	Count
1	LF fwd	No turn	Slightly extend L arm fwd	2
2	Transfer weight to RF	"	Contract L arm over 2 - 5 to end with L hand close to L hip	3
3-5	Slip Chasse LRL	"		4&1
6	RF back, small step	"	Brace L arm towards end of preceding beat, then L arm to side	2
7	Transfer weight to LF	1/8 to L over 7 - 10	Increase tone in L arm	3
8-10	RF to side to chasse RLR End in Fan Position		Slightly extend L arm. L hand still	4&1

Study Alignment   1 To wall   2 To centre   3 - 5 Backing centre
6 To centre   7 - 10 Gradually turn over 7 - 10 to end facing DW

OPEN HIP TWIST (continued)

LADY	Foot Position	Amount of Turn	Count
1	RF back	No turn	2
2	Transfer weight to LF	,,	3
3-5	Fwd Lock RLR	,,	4&1
6	LF fwd	1/4 to R	2
7	RF fwd and slightly across, then turn to end RF back	1/8 to L Body turns less then a further 1/2	3
8-10	Bwd Lock LRL End in Fan Position	Body completes turn	4&1

Study Alignment   1 To wall   2 - 5 To centre   6 Down LOD (RF pointing DW)   7 DC. End backing DC   8 - 10 DC

Amount of Turn   See SPECIAL Note on page 17

On step 6 turn is commenced towards end of previous beat of music

Notes

1   In response to Man's lead Lady brings her weight well fwd on 5, responding to Man's increased tome in his L arm with matching tone in her R arm

2   Turn on 6 is initiated from the hips, which are turned more than the upper body

OPEN HIP TWIST (continued)

Precedes   All ended in Open Position

        (L)   Open Basic Movement - Spot or Switch Turn to L (Lady to R) - RF Time Step - Three Cha Cha Chas Fwd - Hockey Stick - Closed Hip Twist - Open Hip Twist - Spiral - Curl - RF Cuban Break - Split Cuban Break commenced with LF - Chase

        (F)   Advanced Hip Twist - Turkish Towel - Follow My Leader

Follows   **(L&F)**   Alemana - Hockey Stick

Follow from steps 1 - 6

        (F)   7 - 10 Hip Twist Spiral

Alternative Finishing Positions and their Follows

1   **Open Position**

        (Man turn 3/8 L over 7 - 10)

        (L)   Open Basic Movement - 1.2 Open Basic Movement into Three Cha Cha Chas Back or 1 - 5 Open Basic Movement into Natural Top - LF Time Step - Alemana - Open Hip Twist - Curl - LF Cuban Break - Split Cuban Break commenced with LF - Chase

        (F)   Turkish Towel - Sweetheart - Follow My Leader

2   **Open CPP**

        (As 7 - 10 of Closed Hip Twist ended in Open CPP)

        (L&F)   New York to LSP - Spot or Switch Turn to R (Lady to L) - Underarm Turn to L - 4 - 9 Three Cha Cha Chas Fwd in LSP - LF Cuban Break - Split Cuban Break commenced with LF

3   **Contact Position**

        (Man turn 1/2 L over 7 - 10 dancing the chasse side and slightly fwd. Lady 3/4 L over 7 - 10 dancing the chasse with LF behind RF as Cuban Cross. Attain normal hold on 10)

        (L&F)   6 -10 or 6 - 15 Reverse Top

17 REVERSE TOP (L&F)

Commence in Contact Position

MAN	Foot Position	Amount of Turn	Lead	Count
1	RF to side and slightly fwd	Up to three complete turns over 1 - 15	Weight change	2
2	Swivel on ball of LF, ending LF in front of RF (Cuban Cross)		"	3
3	RF to side and slightly fwd		"	4
4-15	Repeat 2 & 3 six times		"	&1 2.3 4&1 2.3 4&1

Study Alignment   Commence facing DW End facing DW when maximum turn is used

REVERSE TOP (continued)

LADY	Foot Position	Amount of Turn	Count
1	LF behind RF (Cuban Cross)	Up to three complete turns over 1 - 15	2
2	RF back and slightly to side		3
3-5	LF back, toe turned out, to chasse LRL		4&1
6	RF back and slightly to side		2
7	LF behind RF (Cuban Cross)		3
8-10	RF back and slightly to side to chasse RLR		4&1
11-15	Repeat 1 - 5		2.3 4&1

Study Alignment   Commence backing DW End backing DW if maximum turn is made

REVERSE TOP (continued)

Notes

1   Throughout the Reverse Top Man and Lady rotate around Man's L toe which remains in place

2   Because of the continuous turn the knees will not straighten fully until step 15, therefore only a slight, natural hip movement is used

Precedes   **(L&F)**   Natural Opening Out Movement (Man turns 1/8 L over 3 - 5, placing LF in front of RF as Cuban Cross, to chasse LRL. Lady turns an additional 1/8 L over 3 - 5 to end RF back and slightly to side)

Into steps 6 - 10 or 6 - 15

The following Precedes end in Contact Position with Man RF side and slightly fwd (Lady LF back, tow turned out)

(L)   Closed Basic Movement - Closed Hip Twist - Open Hip Twist - Spiral - Curl
(F)   Advanced Hip Twist

Follows   **(L&F)**   Closed or Open Basic Movement - Fan

From step 10   **(L&F)**   Opening Out from Reverse Top - Aida - 6 - 10 Spiral (having lead Lady into her spiral turn on 10 of Reverse Top)

NOTES

18   OPENING OUT FROM REVERSE TOP (L&F)

Commence in Contact Position

MAN	Foot Position	Amount of Turn	Lead	Count
1	RF to side and slightly fwd	1/8 to L	Weight change	2
2	LF in front of RF (Cuban Cross)	1/8 to L	Increase tone in L arm. Release R hand hold	3
3-5	RF to side to chasse RLR End in Fan Position	1/8 to L over 3 - 5	Slightly extend L arm. L hand still	4&1

Study Alignment   Commence facing wall   1 Facing DW   2 Facing LOD
3 - 5 Continue to turn to end facing DC

Note   On 4 move LF towards instep of RF, toe turned out

LADY	Foot Position	Amount of Turn	Count
1	LF behind RF (Cuban Cross)	5/8 to L over 1 - 5	2
2	RF back and slightly to side		3
3-5	LF back, toe turned out, to chasse LRL End LF back in Fan Position		4&1

Study Alignment   Commence backing wall Turn over 1 - 5 to end DC against LOD

Precedes   **(L&F)**   1 - 10 or 6 - 10 Reverse Top

Follows   **(L&F)**   Alemana - Hockey Stick

19   AIDA (L&F)

Commence in Contact Position

MAN	Foot Position	Amount of Turn	Lead	Count
1	RF back	1/8 to R	Increase tone in L arm. Release R hand hold	2
2	LF back in LSP	1/8 to R	Slightly lower L arm and turn it with body over 2 - 5	3
3-5	Bwd Lock in LSP, RLR	No turn		4&1

Study Alignment   Commence facing wall   1 DC   2 - 5 Down LOD

LADY	Foot Position	Amount of Turn	Count
1	LF back	1/8 to L	2
2	RF back to LSP	1/8 to L	3
3-5	Bwd Lock in LSP, LRL	No turn	4&1

Study Alignment   Commence backing wall   1 DW   2 - 5 Down LOD

AIDA (continued)

			Count
Precedes	**(L&F)**	1 - 10 or 6 - 10 Reverse Top - Hand to Hand to RSP - Three Cha Cha Chas Fwd in RSP, ended facing partner	

Endings **(L&F)**

1 **Rock and Spot Turn**

	Count
Transfer weight fwd to LF in LSP (Lady RF)	2
Transfer weight back to RF in LSP (Lady LF)	3
LF fwd, small step, in LSP to Lock chasse Fwd LRL (Lady RLR)	4&1
RF fwd and slightly across (having turned 1/2 towards end of previous beat of music) into a Spot or Switch Turn to L (Lady to R) completing 1.1/4 turns	2.3.4&1

2 **Switch and Underarm Turn to Right**

	Count
LF to side, having turned 1/4 L to face partner towards end of preceding beat of music (Lady RF side, having turned 1/4 to R)	2
Transfer weight to RF (Lady LF)	3
Compact Chasse LRL (Lady RLR)	4&1
Underarm Turn to R RL RLR (Lady LR LRL)	2.3.4&1

Development

(L&F) The Aida may follow 5 of Curl or Spiral. Man's steps remain unchanged
Lady 1 LF fwd (1/8 L) 2 RF fwd in line with LF to end RF back in LSP 3 - 5 Back Lock in LSP, LRL

20   SPIRAL TURNS (including Spiral, Curl and Rope Spinning)

A spiral turn is danced by the Lady and is a turn made on RF turning L or on LF turning R, allowing the other foot to cross in front without weight. Normally a spiral turn will end with ankles crossed although the cross in the Curl is looser

SPIRAL (L&F)

Commence in Closed Position

MAN	Foot Position	Amount of Turn	Lead	Count
1	LF to side or fwd in RSP	Slight body turn to R	Increase tone and lower L arm to R at chest level. Widen R arm in hold to R side	2
2	Transfer weight to RF		Retain tone in arms	3
3-5	Compact Chasse LRL	Slight body turn to L to normal position	Return arms to normal position over 3 & 4. Raise L hand above Lady's R shoulder to circle anti-clockwise on 5	4&1
6	RF back		L arm to L side lowering L hand to waist level	2
7	Transfer weight to LF	1/8 to L over 7 - 10	Increase tone in L arm	3
8-10	RF to side to chasse RLR End in Fan Position		Slightly extend L arm. L hand still	4&1

Study Alignment   1 - 5 Facing wall   6 To centre   7 - 10 Gradually turn to end facing DW

Note   If preferred the Man may keep his fingers lightly in contact with Lady's waist as she dances her spiral turn on 5

SPIRAL (continued)

LADY	Foot Position	Amount of Turn	Count
1	RF back in RSP	1/2 to R	2
2	Transfer weight to LF		3
3-5	RF fwd and slightly across LF in front of Man to chasse RLR, then turn underarm, allowing LF to cross in front without weight (Spiral turn)	1/4 to L between 2 & 3 then a further 7/8 on 5	4&1
6	LF fwd	1/8 to L	2
7	RF fwd and slightly across, then turn to end RF back	1/8 to L, then a further 1/2 Body turns less	3
8-10	Bwd Lock LRL End in Fan Position	Body completes turn	4&1

Study Alignment   1 To centre   2 To wall   3 - 5 Down LOD. End facing DW   6 Down LOD   7 DC. End backing DC   8 - 10 DC

Amount of Turn See SPECIAL NOTE on page 17

On step 1 turn is commenced towards end of preceding beat of music

Footwork	On 5 turn is made on ball of RF with foot flat (T of LF). Turn could also be made on R toe with heel well off the floor
Alternative Method	Lady may use an Extended Forward Walk on 5

SPIRAL (continued)

Precedes	**(L&F)**	Natural Top - Alemana - Rope Spinning
		(On Alemana and Rope Spinning Man turns body slightly R on 8, leading Lady fwd towards R side. Lady LF fwd in line with RF to chasse LRL. Man LF slightly leftwards on 7)
Into steps 6 - 10		(Leading Lady to dance her spiral turn L when she has placed her preceding step. Lady 5/8 L on spiral turn)
	(L&F)	Hand to Hand to RSP - 1 - 10 Reverse Top - 1 - 5 Cross Basic
Follows	**(L&F)**	Alemana - Hockey Stick

UNDERTURNED SPIRAL

An alternative method of dancing the Spiral is for Man to turn 1/8 L over 7 - 10, dancing a Fwd Lock DW to end in Open Position (Lady 3/4 L after she has placed step 5, to end in Tandem Position, facing wall. 6 LF fwd, DW 7 RF fwd in line with LF, DW then continue to turn 1/2 to end with RF back 8 - 10 Bwd Lock LRL, DW

SPIRAL (continued)

Alternative Finishing Positions and their Follows

1   **Open Position**

(Man turns 3/8 L over 7 - 10)

(L)	Open Basic Movement - 1.2 Open Basic into Three Cha Cha Chas Back or 1 - 5 Open Basic Movement into Natural Top - LF Time Step - Alemana - Open Hip Twist - Curl - LF Cuban Break - Split Cuban Break commenced with LF - Chase
(F)	Turkish Towel - Sweetheart - Follow My Leader

2   **Open CPP**

(L&F)	New York to LSP - Spot or Switch Turn to R (Lady to L) - Underarm Turn to L - 4 - 9 Three Cha Cha Chas Fwd in LSP - LF Cuban Break - Split Cuban Break commenced with LF

3   **Contact Position**

(Man turn 5/8 L over 7 - 10 dancing the chasse side and slightly fwd, overturning Lady, keeping fingers lightly in contact with Lady's waist throughout as she turns within the circle of his R arm. On 6 lower arms to normal position. Lady makes a complete turn L over 6 - 10, dancing the chasse with LF behind RF as Cuban Cross. This is known as the Close Spiral

(L&F)	6 - 10 or 6 - 15 Reverse Top

Development

(L&F)	Dance 1 - 5 of Spiral and continue with Aida as explained on page 85

4   **Left Side Position**

(Man no turn over 7 to 10 leading Lady to overturn on 7, lowering L arm and taking it slightly fwd. Lady turns an additional 1/8 to L on 7 using a loosely crossed spiral action, both dance a fwd Lock on 8 - 10)

(L&F)	Spot or Switch Turn to R (Lady to L) - New York to LSP (no turn on first step) - 4 - 9 Three Cha Cha Chas Fwd in LSP - LF Cuban Break commencing with LF (Lady RF)

CURL (L&F)

Commence in Open Position

MAN	Foot Position	Amount of Turn	Lead	Count
1	LF fwd	No turn	Slightly extend L arm fwd	2
2	Transfer weight to RF	"	Contract L arm	3
3-5	Compact Chasse LRL	"	Gradually raise L hand to above Lady's R shoulder to circle anti-clockwise on 5	4&1
6-10	Continue with 6 - 10 of Spiral	As 6 - 10 of Spiral	As Spiral	2.3 4&1

Study Alignment   1 To wall   2 To centre   3 - 5 Backing centre
6 - 10 As Spiral

Note   If preferred Man may keep his fingers lightly in contact with Lady's waist as she dances her spiral turn on 5

LADY	Foot Position	Amount of Turn	Count
1	RF back	No turn	2
2	Transfer weight to LF	"	3
3-5	RF fwd Lock to Chasse RLR, then turn allowing LF to cross loosely in front without weight (Spiral turn)	5/8 to L on 5	4&1
6-10	Continue with 6 - 10 of Spiral	As 6 - 10 of Spiral	2.3 4&1

Study Alignment   1 To wall   2 To centre   3 - 5 To centre. End facing DW
6 - 10 As Spiral

Footwork   On step 5 turn is made on ball of RF with foot flat (T of LF)

Precedes, Follows and Alternative Finishing Positions as for Spiral

90

NOTES

ROPE SPINNING (L&F)

The Rope Spinning is commenced during the last step of the preceding figure. Man leads Lady to turn sharply R under raised L arm, inclining and turning his body slightly R, releasing R hand hold

MAN	Foot Position	Amount of Turn	Lead	Count
1	LF to side	Continue to turn body to R	Circle L hand clockwise over head over 1 & 2	2
2	Transfer weight to RF	Turn body slightly to L		3
3-5	Compact Chasse LRL End in LSP	Continue to turn body to L to normal position	L hand to L side. Gradually lower to waist level over 3 - 5	4&1
6	RF back	No turn	Continue to circle L hand clockwise over 6 - 9	2
7	Transfer weight to LF	,,		3
8-10	Compact Chasse RLR End in Closed Position	,,	Take required hold at end of 10	4&1

Study Alignment   1 - 5 Facing wall   6 To centre   7 To wall
8 - 10 Facing wall

Inclination of Body   Continue to incline body R on 1, returning body to normal position over 2 & 3. Incline body slightly L on 6, returning body to normal position on 7

Note on lead   If preferred Man may keep his R hand lightly in contact with Lady as she dances her spiral turn on the preceding step, ending with the back of his hand on her back

ROPE SPINNING (continued)

The Rope Spinning is commenced during the last step of the preceding figure.
Make a complete turn R on LF, body turning less. (Spiral turn).
End on Man's R side facing opposite way

LADY	Foot Position	Amount of Turn	Count
1-5	Two walks fwd RL, then Fwd Lock RLR, circling R behind Man's back. End in LSP	1/2 to R over 1 - 5	2.3.4&1
6-10	Two walks fwd LR, then Fwd Lock LRL, still circling R End in Closed Position	1/2 to R over 6 - 10	2.3.4&1

Study Alignment   Commence facing centre   1 - 5 Gradually curve over 1 - 5
to end to wall   6 - 10 Gradually curve over 6 - 10 to end to centre

Footwork   On preceding step (spiral) turn is made on ball
                                          of LF with foot flat (T of RF)

Precedes   (L&F)   Hand to Hand to LSP (Man Compact Chasse
                                          on 3 - 5 - Alemana - Natural Top - Rope
                                          Spinning

                                          On Alemana and Rope Spinning Man turns
                                          body slightly R on 8 to lead Lady towards his R
                                          side. (Lady LF fwd in line with RF into Fwd
                                          Lock LRL) Man LF slightly leftwards on 7

Follows   (L&F)   Closed or Open Basic Movement - There and
                                          Back - Fan

Alternative Finishing Positions and their Follows

1   **Man and Lady end to side**

                    (L&F)   Hand to Hand to RSP - Side Step to L
                                          commenced with LF - Side Step to R com-
                                          menced with LF - LF Time Step - Cross Basic -
                                          LF Cuban Break - Split Cuban Break com-
                                          menced with LF

ROPE SPINNING (continued)

Alternative Finishing Position and their Follows (continued)

2   **Man and Lady end diagonally fwd in Open CPP**

(Man 1/8 to R on 8 arresting Lady's turn with L hand. Lady 7/8 R over 1 - 8)

(L&F)   New York to LSP - Spot or Switch Turn to R (Lady to L) - Underarm Turn to L - 4 - 9 Three Cha Cha Chas Fwd in LSP - LF Cuban Break - Split Cuban Break commenced with LF

3   **Lady end fwd towards Man's R side**

(Man turns body slightly R on 8 to lead Lady towards his R side. Lady LF fwd in line with RF into Fwd Lock) Man LF slightly leftwards on 7

(L&F)   Natural Opening Out Movement - Closed Hip Twist - Spiral - Rope Spinning

4   **Man and Lady fwd towards partner's R side**

(Man RF fwd in line with LF on 8, into Fwd Lock towards Lady's R side. Lead, foot placement and Lady's steps as position 3) Man may turn up to 1/4 R over 7 - 10, Lady turning up to 1/4 more accordingly

(F)   Advanced Hip Twist - Hip Twist Spiral

NOTES

21   CROSS BASIC (L&F)

Commence in Closed Position

MAN	Foot Position	Amount of Turn	Lead	Count
1	Cross LF in front of RF, toe turned out	1/8 to L	Weight change	2
2	RF back, having moved it slightly rightwards	Continue to turn to L	″	3
3-5	LF to side and slightly fwd to chasse LRL	1/8 to L over 3 - 5	″	4&1
6	Cross RF behind LF, toe turned out	1/8 to L	″	2
7	LF fwd, having moved it slightly leftwards	Continue to turn to L	″	3
8-10	RF to side and slightly back to chasse RLR	1/8 to L over 8 - 10	″	4&1

Study Alignment   Commence facing wall   1 Facing DW   2 DC against LOD   3 - 5 End facing LOD   6 Facing DC   7 DC   8 - 10 End facing centre

Footwork   6 B (heel lowers towards floor)

On 1 & 6 retain pressure into ball of foot as it moves towards the crossed position

Note   Incline body slightly L on 1 & 2 and R on 6 & 7

CROSS BASIC (continued)

LADY	Foot Position	Amount of Turn	Count
1	Cross RF behind LF, toe turned out	1/8 to L	2
2	LF fwd, having moved it slightly leftwards	Continue to turn to L	3
3-5	RF to side and slightly back to chasse RLR	1/8 to L over 3 - 5	4&1
6	Cross LF in front of RF, toe turned out	1/8 to L	2
7	RF back, having moved it slightly rightwards	Continue to turn to L	3
8-10	LF to side and slightly fwd to chasse LRL	1/8 to L over 8 - 10	4&1

Study Alignment   Commence backing wall   1 Backing DW   2 DC against LOD   3 - 5 End backing LOD   6 Backing DC   7 DC   8 - 10 End backing centre

Footwork   1 B (heel lowers towards floor)

On 1 & 6 retain pressure into ball of foot as it moves towards the crossed position

Note   Incline body slightly R on 1 & 2 and L on 6 & 7

CROSS BASIC (continued)

Precedes	**(L&F)**	Closed Basic Movement - New York to RSP ended facing partner - Spot or Switch Turn to L (Lady to R) - Underarm Turn to R - R Side Shoulder to Shoulder ended facing partner - Hand to Hand to LSP - Three Cha Cha Chas Fwd in LSP ended facing partner - Side Step to R commenced with RF - RF Time Step - Alemana - Rope Spinning - Cross Basic - RF Cuban Break - Split Cuban Break commenced with LF
Note		The preceding step is side and slightly back (Lady side and slightly fwd) with Man inclining his body slightly L (Lady R)
Follows	**(L&F)**	Closed Basic Movement - Spot or Switch Turn to R (Lady to L) - Hand to Hand to RSP - Side Step to R or L commenced with LF - There and Back - LF Time Step - Fan - Cross Basic - LF Cuban Break - Split Cuban Break commenced with LF
Note		When not following with another Cross Basic the last chasse is taken to side
Follows to steps 1 - 5		
	(L&F)	Underarm Turn to R (Man continue to turn L on chasse, lessening Lady's turn R) - 6 - 10 of Fan - 6 - 10 of Spiral (having lead Lady to dance a spiral turn on 5)
Notes	1	On the last chasse (8 - 10) Lady may be lead to Fan Position, Open Position or Open CPP, adjusting turn accordingly. Any of the normal follows to these positions may be used
	2	Guapacha timing is often used on this figure
Development	**(F)**	Raise L arm and lead Lady to dance a spiral turn L on 5. Regain normal hold on 8. (Lady 5/8 L on spiral turn, then two fwd steps continuing to turn L (LR) to end RF back and slightly to side facing partner, to continue with the normal 8 - 10 of Cross Basic

22   CUBAN BREAKS (L&F)

Cuban Breaks may be danced at any time when in Closed or Open Position without hold. They may also be danced from Open PP, Open CPP, RSP and LSP

Commencing position and hold according to preceding figure

LEFT FOOT CUBAN BREAK

MAN LADY	Foot Position	Amount of Turn	Count
1	LF fwd and across, toe turned out. Small step	1/8 to R	2
2	Replace weight to RF		&
3	LF to side	1/8 to L	3
4	Replace weight to RF	No turn	&
5-7	Repeat 1 - 3	As 1 - 3	4&1

Study Alignment   Commence facing wall   1 DW against LOD   2 DC
3 - 4 Facing wall   5 - 7 As 1 - 3

RIGHT FOOT CUBAN BREAK

MAN LADY	Foot Position	Amount of Turn	Count
1	RF fwd and across, toe turned out. Small step	1/8 to L	2
2	Replace weight to LF		&
3	RF to side	1/8 to R	3
4	Replace weight to LF	No turn	&
5-7	Repeat 1 - 3	As 1 - 3	4&1

Study Alignment   Commence facing wall   1 DW   2 DC against LOD
3 - 4 Facing wall   5 - 7 As 1 - 3

Footwork   2,4& 6 Ball of foot

NOTES   Beat value of each step 1/2. 1/2. 1/2. 1/2. 1/2. 1/2. 1
                   The Cuban Break maybe danced without turn

CUBAN BREAKS (continued)

Example amalgamation when Cuban Breaks are danced facing partner without hold

Man LF Cuban Break (Lady RF Time Step or 1-5 Closed Basic Movement)
Man RF Cuban Break (Lady accepts the "challenge" and dances a LF Cuban Break)
Man Spot or Switch Turn to R (Lady RF Cuban Break)
Man RF Time Step or 6 - 10 Closed Basic Movement (Lady Spot or switch Turn to R)

SPLIT CUBAN BREAK (L&F)

This figure may be danced in place of the normal Cuban Break and may be commenced with either foot in any of the positions given for the Cuban Breaks

Man or Lady starting with LF

1 - 3	Dance 1 - 3 of the LF Cuban Break LRL	Count 2 & 3
4 - 6	Dance 1 - 3 of the RF Cuban Break RLR	Count 4 & 1

(**Footwork** Ball flat on each step)

A popular way of dancing the Split Cuban Breaks from Open PP or Open CPP is to turn (as in chart) changing hands as in New York. More turn could be made as if dancing the New York with quick timing and using only one step in place of the chasse

When commenced in RSP or LSP typical amalgamations would be:-

	Count
Example 1	
Fan	2.3.4&1
	2.3.4&1
Hockey Stick ended in LSP	2.3.4&1
	2.3.4&1
Man LF Cuban Break (Lady RF Cuban Break)	2&3&4&1
Man RF Cuban Break (Lady LF Cuban Break)	2&3&4&1
New York to LSP (No turn on 1)	2.3.4&1
Spot Turn to L (Lady to R)	2.3.4&1
Example 2	
1.2 of Hand to Hand to RSP	2.3
Three Cha Cha Chas Fwd in RSP	4&1,2&3,
	4&1
Split Cuban Break (Man commencing RF, Lady LF)	2&3, 4&1
New York to RSP (No turn on 1) End facing partner	2.3.4&1

23 CHASE (L&F)

Commence in Open Position. No hold

MAN	Foot Position	Amount of Turn	Lead	Count
1	LF fwd in line with RF or LF as appropriate, then turn to end LF back in TP, Lady behind	1/2 to R	Visual	2
2	Close RF to LF without weight	No turn	”	3
3-5	Fwd Lock RLR	”	”	4&1
6	LF fwd in line with RF or LF as appropriate, then turn to end LF back in TP, Lady in front	1/2 to R	”	2
7	Transfer weight to RF	No turn	”	3
8-10	Fwd Lock LRL following Lady	”	”	4&1
11	RF fwd in line with RF or LF as appropriate, then turn to end RF back in TP, Lady behind	1/2 to L	”	2
12	Transfer weight to LF	No turn	”	3
13-15	Fwd Lock RLR	”	”	4&1
16	LF fwd in line with RF or LF as appropriate, then turn to end LF back in TP, Lady in front	1/2 to R	”	2
17	Close RF to LF without weight	No turn	”	3
18-20	Fwd Lock RLR End in Open Position	”	”	4&1

Study Alignment   1   To wall. End backing wall   2   Facing centre
3 - 5   To centre   6   To centre. End backing centre   7 - 10   To wall
11 To wall. End backing wall   12 - 15 To centre   16 To centre. End backing
centre   17 Facing wall   18 - 20 To wall

CHASE (continued)

LADY	Foot Position	Amount of Turn	Count
1	RF back	No turn	2
2	Transfer weight to LF in TP, Man in front	,,	3
3-5	Fwd Lock RLR, following Man	,,	4&1
6	LF fwd in line with LF or RF as appropriate, then turn to end LF back in TP, Man behind	1/2 to R	2
7	Transfer weight to RF	No turn	3
8-10	Fwd Lock LRL	,,	4&1
11	RF fwd in line with LF or RF as appropriate, then turn to end RF back in TP, Man in front	1/2 to L	2
12	Transfer weight to LF	No turn	3
13-15	Fwd Lock RLR, following Man	,,	4&1
16	LF fwd in line with LF or RF as appropriate then turn to end LF back in TP, Man behind	1/2 to R	2
17	Transfer weight to RF	No turn	3
18	Close LF near to RF	3/8 to R	4
19	Replace weight to RF	1/8 to R	&
20	LF back	No turn	1

Study Alignment   1 To wall   2 - 5 To centre   6 To centre. End backing centre   7 - 10 To wall   11 To wall. End backing wall   12 - 15 To centre 16 To centre. End backing centre   17 To wall   18 Facing DC against LOD 19 Facing centre   20 To wall

On steps 18.19 turn is commenced towards end of previous beat of music

CHASE (continued)

LADY (continued)

Precedes

All ended in Open Position

(L&F)   Open Basic Movement - Spot or Switch Turn to
L (Lady to R) - RF Time Step - Three Cha Cha
Chas Fwd - Hockey Stick - Closed Hip Twist -
Open Hip Twist - Spiral - Curl - RF Cuban
Break -Split Cuban Break commenced with LF -
Turkish Towel - Follow My Leader

Follows   **(L&F)**   Open Basic Movement - 1.2 Open Basic Move-
ment into Three Cha Cha Chas Back or 1 - 5
Open Basic Movement into Natural Top - LF
Time Step - Alemana - Open Hip Twist - Curl -
Sweetheart

(F)   Turkish Towel - Follow My Leader

NOTES

Commence in Closed Position

MAN	Foot Position	Amount of Turn	Lead	Count
1	LF fwd in RSP	Slight body turn to R	Increase tone and lower L arm to R at chest level. Widen R arm in hold to R side	2
2	Transfer weight to RF		Retain tone in arms	3
3-5	LF behind RF (Cuban Cross) to chasse LRL	1/8 to L (LF), body turns less	Retain tone and return arms to normal position, slightly to R	4&1
6	RF back	Body completes turn	Towards end of preceding beat lower L arm to a Promenade shape, then L arm to L side	2
7	Transfer weight to LF	1/8 to L over 7 - 10	Increase tone in L arm. Release R hand hold	3
8-10	RF to side to chasse RLR End in Fan Position		Slightly extend L arm, L hand still	4&1

Study Alignment   1 To wall   2 To centre   3 - 5 LF Pointing DW
6 DC against LOD   7 DW   8 - 10 Gradually turn to end facing LOD

Notes   1   Steps 3 is similar to a Pressed Backward Walk but the heel is not lowered and the knee remains flexed

2   Step 5 is a Pressed Backward Walk

3   A Ronde Chasse may be danced in place of 3 - 5

ADVANCED HIP TWIST (continued)

LADY	Foot Position	Amount of Turn	Count
1	RF back in RSP	1/2 to R	2
2	Transfer weight to LF		3
3-5	RF fwd in line with LF to Man's R side to chasse RLR	5/8 to L	4&1
6	LF fwd passing in front of Man	1/4 to R	2
7	RF fwd and slightly across, then turn to end RF back	1/8 to L then a further 1/2 Body turns less	3
8-10	Bwd Lock LRL End in Fan Position	Body completes turn	4&1

Study Alignment   1 To centre   2 To wall   3 - 5 DC against LOD   6 DC, R toe pointing LOD   7 To centre. End backing centre   8 - 10 To centre

Amount of Turn   See SPECIAL NOTE on page 17

On steps 1, 3 and 6 turn is commenced towards end of previous beat of music

Notes   1   Step 3 is similar to a Pressed Forward Walk but the heel is not lowered and the knee remains flexed

2   Step 5 is a Pressed Forward Walk

3   Turn on 6 is initiated from the hips, which are turned more than the upper body

4   A Twist Chasse may be danced in place of 3 - 5

ADVANCED HIP TWIST (continued)

Precedes	**(F)**	Natural Top - Alemana - Rope Spinning

Man's preceding chasse RF fwd in line with LF towards Lady's R side. (On Alemana and Rope Spinning Man turns body slightly R on 8 to lead Lady towards his R side Lady LF fwd in line with RF to chasse LRL Man LF slightly leftwards on 7) Up to 1/4 turn R may be made on this preceding chasse

Follows	**(F)**	Alemana - Hockey Stick

Alternative Finishing Positions and their Follows

1   **Open Position**
(Man turn 3/8 L over 7 - 10)

(F)   Open Basic Movement - 1.2 Open Basic Movement into Three Cha Cha Chas Back or 1-5 Open Basic Movement into Natural Top - LF Time Step - Alemana - Open Hip Twist - Curl - LF Cuban Break - Split Cuban Break commenced with LF - Chase - Turkish Towel - Sweetheart - Follow My Leader

2   **Open CPP**
(As 7 - 10 of Closed Hip Twist ended in Open CPP)

(F)   New York to LSP - Spot or Switch Turn to R (Lady to L) - Underarm Turn to L - 4 - 9 Three Cha Cha Chas Fwd in LSP - LF Cuban Break - Split Cuban Break commenced with LF

3   **Contact Position**
(Man 1/2 L over 7 - 10 dancing the chasse side and slightly fwd. Lady 3/4 L over 7 - 10 dancing the chasse with LF behind RF as Cuban Cross). Normal hold retained throughout

(F)   6 - 10 or 6 - 15 Reverse Top

Developments

1   Man may use a "Press Line" on 1 by making a slight swivel to R on RF and placing LF fwd on ball of foot with pressure but with part weight

2   The Advanced Hip Twist may also be danced following the Alemana with R to R hand hold, changing to L to R hand hold on 7 of the Advanced Hip Twist

NOTES

25   HIP TWIST SPIRAL (F)

Commenced in Closed Position

MAN	Foot Position	Amount of Turn	Lead	Count
1	LF fwd in RSP	Slight body turn to R	Increase tone and lower L arm to R at chest level. Widen R arm hold to R side	2
2	Transfer weight to RF		Retain tone in arms	3
3-5	Ronde Chasse ended in PP, LRL	1/8 to L (LF), body turns less on 3. Body completes turn on 4. No turn on 5	Retain tone and return arms to normal position slightly to R on 3. Retain tone in arms on 4. Lower L arm to a Promenade shape on 5	4&1
6	RF back	No turn	L arm slightly to L	2
7	Transfer weight to LF	1/4 to L over 7 - 10	L arm slightly to L then raise L hand above Lady's R shoulder to circle anti-clockwise	3
8-10	Fwd Lock RLR End RF diag fwd in Open CPP		Continue to circle L hand anti-clockwise, gradually lowering to L side just below shoulder level	4&1

Study Alignment   1 To wall   2 To centre   3 Pointing DW   4 Facing DW
5 Facing DW   6 DC against LOD   7 Almost LOD   8 - 10 Gradually turn
to end facing DC, moving along LOD

LADY	Foot Position	Amount of Turn	Count
1	RF back in RSP	1/2 to R	2
2	Transfer weight to LF		3
3-5	Twist Chasse ended RF diag fwd in PP	5/8 to L on 3, 1/4 to R on 4 No turn on 5	4&1
6	LF fwd passing in front of Man	No turn	2
7	RF fwd in line with LF, then turn underarm allowing LF to cross in front without weight (Spiral turn)	1 turn to L	3
8	LF fwd	1/8 to L	4
9	Close RF to LF	1/2 to L	&
10	LF diag fwd in Open CPP	1/8 to L	1

Study Alignment   1 To centre   2 To wall   3 DC against LOD   4 - 6 DC   7 DC to end facing DC   8 To centre   9 Facing wall   10 Facing DW, moving along LOD

Footwork   On 7 turn is made on ball of RF with foot flat (T of LF)

On steps 1,3,4 and 9 turn is commenced towards end of previous beat of music

Notes	**1**	3 is a Pressed Forward Walk. An Extended Forward Walk may be used on 7
	2	Turn on 3 is initiated from the hips, which are turned more than the upper body
Precedes	**(F)**	As for Advanced Hip Twist
Follows	**(F)**	New York to LSP - Spot or Switch Turn to R (Lady to L) - Underarm Turn to L - 4 - 9 Three Cha Cha Chas Fwd in LSP - LF Cuban Break - Split Cuban Break commenced with LF
Development		7 - 10 may be danced following 1 - 6 of Open Hip Twist

Commence in Open Position. R to R hand hold

MAN	Foot Position	Amount of Turn	Lead	Count
1-7	As Alemana from Open Position	1 - 7 No turn	1 - 7 As Alemana with R to R hand hold	2.3.4&1 2.3
8-10	Compact Chasse RLR End RF to side in L Shadow Position, Lady behind	1/4 to L over 8 - 10	Lower R arm, gradually taking it behind back. On 10 take L to L hand hold slightly to L side at hip level	4&1
11	LF back in LSP, toe turned out	No turn	L arm slightly fwd	2
12	Transfer weight to RF	''	R arm slightly to R	3
13-15	LF to side to chasse LRL End in R Shadow Position, Lady behind	''	Gradually reverse arm positions to L arm behind back, R hand slightly to R side	4&1
16	RF back in RSP, toe turned out	''	R arm slightly fwd	2
17	Transfer weight to LF	''	L arm slightly to L	3
18-20	RF to side to chasse RLR End in L Shadow Position, Lady behind	''	Gradually reverse arm positions to R arm behind back, L hand slightly to L side	4&1

TURKISH TOWEL (continued)

MAN	Foot Position	Amount of Turn	Lead	Count
21-25	As 11 - 15 End in RSP	No turn	As 11-15 releasing L hand hold on 23. On 25 R arm down and fwd then release R to R hand hold	2.3.4&1
26-30	As 6 - 10 of Hockey Stick End in Open Position	As 6 - 10 of Hockey Stick	Take required hold on 1 of following figure	2.3.4&1

Study Alignment 1 To wall   2 To centre   3 - 5 Backing centre   6 To centre
7 To wall   8 - 10 Gradually turn to end facing LOD   11 Against LOD
12 Down LOD   13 -15 Facing LOD   16 Against LOD   17 Down LOD
18 - 20 Facing LOD   21 - 25 As 11 - 15   26 DC against LOD   27 - 30 DW

TURKISH TOWEL (continued)

LADY	Foot Position	Amount of Turn	Count
1-7	As Alemana from Open Position	No turn on 1 - 5, 1/2 to R on 6, 3/8 on R to 7	2.3.4&1 2.3
8-10	Fwd Lock LRL, moving behind Man's back to end LF side and slightly fwd in L Shadow Position, Man in front	3/8 to R over 8 - 10	4&1
11	RF fwd in LSP, toe turned out	No turn	2
12	Transfer weight to LF	"	3
13-15	RF to side to chasse RLR, moving behind Man's back to R Shadow Position, Man in front	"	4&1
16	LF fwd in RSP, toe turned out	"	2
17	Transfer weight to RF	"	3
18-20	LF to side to chasse LRL, moving behind Man's back to L Shadow Position, Man in front	"	4&1
21-24	As 11 - 14	As 11 - 14	2.3.4&
25	RF fwd and slightly to side in RSP, then turn on RF allowing LF to cross in front without weight (Spiral)	3/4 to L	1
26-30	As 6 - 10 of Hockey Stick. End in Open Position	As 6 - 10 of Hockey Stick	2.3.4&1

TURKISH TOWEL (continued)

LADY (continued)

Study Alignment 1 To wall 2 - 5 To centre 6 To wall 7 DC against LOD 8 - 10 Gradually curve to end down LOD 11 Down LOD 12 Against LOD 13 - 15 Facing LOD 16 Down LOD 17 Against LOD 18 - 20 Facing LOD 21 - 24 As 11 - 14 25 Down LOD End facing wall 26 - 30 DW

FOOTWORK On 25 turn is made on ball of RF with foot flat (T of LF)

Precedes		All ended in Open Position taking R to R hand hold at end of preceding step
	(F)	Open Basic Movement - Spot or Switch Turn to L (Lady to R) - RF Time Step - Three Cha Cha Chas Fwd - Hockey Stick - Closed Hip Twist - Open Hip Twist - Spiral - Curl - RF Cuban Break - Split Cuban Break commenced with LF - Chase - Advanced Hip Twist - Follow My Leader
Follows	**(F)**	Open Basic Movement - 1.2 Open Basic Movement into Three Cha Cha Chas Back or 1- 5 Open Basic Movement into Natural Top - LF Time Step - Alemana - Open Hip Twist - Curl - LF Cuban Break - Split Cuban Break commenced with LF - Chase - Sweetheart - Follow My Leader

Alternative Hold

1	When double hand hold is achieved on 10, slightly raise R arm and lower L arm. Reverse these arm positions over 13 - 15 (L arm slightly raised and R arm lowered) Reverse arm positions again over 18 - 20. Release hold with L hand on 23, lowering R hand over 23 - 25. Continue as chart
2	One hand hold (R to R) may be used for 1 - 25, in which case Man would not take L hand behind back

27 SWEETHEART (F)

Commence in Open Position. R to R hand hold

MAN	Foot Position	Amount of Turn	Lead	Count
1	LF fwd	No turn	Slightly extend R arm fwd	2
2	Transfer weight to RF	"	Slightly contract R arm	3
3-5	LF to side to chasse LRL End in RSP	"	Gradually raise R arm to R side. On 5 take L to L hand hold, both arms raised, hands eye level Retain double hold, arms toned and raised	4&1
6	RF fwd in RSP, toe turned out	Slight body turn to R	Lower L arm slightly fwd	2
7	Transfer weight to LF	No turn	Retain arm position	3
8-10	RF to side to chasse RLR moving behind Lady's back to end in LSP	Return body to previous position	Return L arm to previous position	4&1
11	LF fwd in LSP, toe turned out	Slight body turn to L	Lower R arm slightly fwd	2
12	Transfer weight to RF	No turn	Retain arm position	3
13-15	LF to side to chasse LRL moving behind Lady's back to end in RSP	Return body to previous position	Return R arm to previous position	4&1

SWEETHEART (continued)

MAN (continued)

MAN	Foot Position	Amount of Turn	Lead	Count
	Retain RSP for 16 - 26			
16	RF back	"	Weight change	2
17	Transfer weight to LF	No turn	"	3
18-20	Fwd Runs or Fwd Lock RLR	"	"	4&1
21	LF fwd	"	"	2
22	Transfer weight to RF	"	"	3
23-25	Bwd Runs or Bwd Lock LRL	"	"	4&1
26	RF back	"	"	2
27	Close LF to RF	"	Slightly extend L arm to L side and release L to L hand hold	3
28-30	RF to side to chasse RLR End in Fan Position	"	Move R arm slightly across body. Change to L to R hand hold on step 30	4&1

Study Alignment 1 To wall 2 To centre 3 - 5 Facing wall 6 To wall 7 To centre 8 - 10 Facing wall 11 To wall 12 To centre 13 - 15 Facing wall 16 To centre 17 -21 To wall 22 - 26 To centre 27 To wall 28 - 30 Facing wall

SWEETHEART (continued)

LADY	Foot Position	Amount of Turn	Count
1	RF back	No turn	2
2	Transfer weight to LF	Commence to Turn to L	3
3-5	Fwd Lock RLR to end RF back and slightly to side in RSP	1/2 to L over 3 - 5	4&1
6	LF back in RSP, toe turned out	Slight body turn to L	
7	Transfer weight to RF	No turn	3
8-10	LF to side to chasse LRL to end LF back and slightly to side in LSP	Return body to previous position	4&1
11	RF back in LSP, toe turned out	Slight body turn to R	2
12	Transfer weight to LF	No turn	3
13-15	RF to side to chasse RLR to end RF back and slightly to side in RSP	Return body to previous position	4&1
16	LF back	No turn	2
17	Transfer weight to RF	"	3
18-20	Fwd Runs or Fwd Lock LRL	"	4&1
21	RF fwd	"	2
22	Transfer weight to LF	"	3
23-25	Bwd Runs or Bwd Lock RLR	"	4&1

LADY (continued)

LADY	Foot Position	Amount of Turn	Count
26	LF back	No turn	2
27	RF fwd and slightly across LF	Commence to turn to R	3
28-30	LF to side and slightly back to chasse LRL End with LF back in Fan Position	1/4 to R over 28 - 30	4&1

Study Alignment   1 To wall   2 To centre   3 - 5 Gradually turn to end backing centre   6 To centre   7 To wall   8 - 10 Facing wall   11 To centre   12 To wall   13 - 15 Facing wall   16 To centre   17 - 21 To wall   22 - 26 To centre   27 To wall   28 - 30 Gradually turn to end down LOD

Precedes   All ended in Open Position taking R to R hand hold at end of preceding step

(F)   Open Basic Movement - Spot or Switch Turn to L (Lady to R) - RF Time Step - Three Cha Chas Fwd - Hockey Stick - Closed Hip Twist - Open Hip Twist - Spiral - Curl - RF Cuban Break - Split Cuban Break commenced with LF - Chase - Advanced Hip Twist - Follow My Leader

Follows   **(F)**   Alemana - Hockey Stick

Alternative Hold   R Shadow Hold may be achieved on 5 (L to L hand hold, R hand on Lady's back). Retain this hold for 6 & 7, gradually changing to L Shadow Hold over 8 - 10 (R to R hand hold L hand on Lady's back). Retain hold for 11 & 12, gradually changing to R shadow Hold again over 13 - 15. Retain R Shadow Hold, changing to L to R hand hold on 28

Commence in Open Position

MAN	Foot Position	Amount of Turn	Lead	Count
1-5	1 - 5 as Alemana from Open Position	No turn	As 1 - 5 Alemana On 5 commence to circle L hand clockwise	2 3 4&1
6	RF behind LF (Cuban Cross)	3/8 to R over 6.7	Continue to circle L hand clockwise. Release R hand hold	2
7	LF side		Gradually lower L arm behind back cover 7 & 8	3
8-10	Fwd Lock in TP, Lady behind, RLR	1/4 to R over 8 - 10	Release L hand hold on 9, then visual	4&1
11	LF fwd	3/8 to L over 11.12	Visual	2
12	RF fwd		"	3
13-15	Fwd Lock in TP, Lady in front, LRL	3/8 to L over 13 - 15	No lead	4&1
16	RF fwd	3/8 to R over 16.17	"	2
17	LF fwd		"	3
18-20	Fwd Lock in TP, Lady behind, RLR	3/8 to R over 18 - 20	Visual	4&1
21	LF fwd	3/8 to L over 21.22	"	2
22	RF fwd		"	3
23-25	Fwd Lock in TP, Lady in front, LRL	3/8 to L over 23 - 25	No lead	4&1

FOLLOW MY LEADER (continued)

MAN	Foot Position	Amount of Turn	Lead	Count
26	RF back	No turn	No lead	2
27	Transfer weight to LF	,,	,,	3
28-30	RF to side to chasse RLR End in Open Position	,,	Take required hold at end of figure	4&1

Study Alignment   1 To wall   2 To centre   3 - 5 Backing centre   6.7 End DC against LOD   8 - 10 End DC   11.12 End against LOD   13 - 15 End DW   16.17 End against LOD   18 - 20 End DC   21.22 End against LOD 23 - 25 End DW   26 DC against LOD   27 DW   28 - 30 Facing DW

LADY	Foot Position	Amount of Turn	Count
1-5	1 - 5 as Alemana from Open Position	No turn on 1 - 4. 1/8 to R on 5	2 3 4&1
6	LF fwd under raised arms	3/8 to R	2
7	RF fwd	3/8 to R	3
8-10	Fwd Lock in TP behind Man, LRL	1/4 to R over 8 - 10	4&1
11	RF fwd	3/8 to L over 11.12	2
12	LF fwd		3
13-15	Fwd Lock in TP in front of Man, RLR	3/8 to L over 13 - 15	4&1
16	LF fwd	3/8 to R over 16.17	2
17	RF fwd		3
18-20	Fwd Lock in TP behind Man, LRL	3/8 to R over 18 - 20	4&1
21	RF fwd	3/8 to L over 21.22	2
22	LF fwd		3
23-25	Fwd Lock in TP in front of Man, RLR	3/8 to L over 23 - 25	4&1
26	LF fwd	3/8 to R over 26.27	2
27	RF fwd		3
28	Close LF near to RF	1 1/8 to R over 28.29	4
29	Close RF to LF		&
30	LF to side. End in Open Position	No turn	1

Study Alignment   1 To wall   2 - 4 To centre   5 DC   6 To wall   7 DC against LOD   8 - 10 End DC   11.12 End against LOD   13 - 15 End DW 16.17 End against LOD   18 - 20 End DC   21.22 End against LOD 23 - 25 End DW   26.27 End against LOD   28.29 End facing DC against LOD   30 Facing DC against LOD

FOLLOW MY LEADER (continued)

Lady (continued)

On step 6,7, 28 & 29 turn is commenced towards end of previous beat of music. Most of the turn over steps 28. 29 is made on RF on step 28

Note   Lady could step back LF on last step

Note   **Man & Lady**

Steps 8 - 25 have a "figure eight" pattern. When turning R Man takes slightly smaller steps. (Lady is following him and her circumference of circle is larger). When turning L the roles are reversed and the Lady takes slightly smaller steps.

Precedes

All ended in Open Position

(F)   Open Basic - Spot or Switch Turn to L (Lady to R) - RF Time Step - Three Cha Cha Chas Fwd - Hockey Stick - Closed, Open or Advanced Hip Twist - Spiral - Curl - RF Cuban Break - Split Cuban Break commenced with LF - Turkish Towel - Chase

Into steps 6 - 30

(F)   1 - 10 Natural Top

Follows

(F)   Open Basic Movement - 1.2 Open Basic Movement into Three Cha Cha Chas Back or 1-5 Open Basic Movement into Natural Top - LF Time Step - Alemana - Open Hip Twist - Curl - LF Cuban Break - Split Cuban Break commenced with LF - Turkish Towel - Sweetheart - Chase

Alternative Finishing Position

Man and Lady dance a Fwd Lock towards partner's R side on steps 28 - 30. Man turns body slightly R to invite Lady towards his R side. (Lady 1/8 to R over 28 - 30) Man LF slightly leftwards on 27

Follow with Advanced Hip Twist or Hip Twist Spiral

29   FOOT CHANGES (F)

Many figures may be danced with Man and Lady using the same foot, having achieved Right Side, Right Shadow or Tandem Position, the Man having danced a Foot Change

The following syllabus figures may be used in a short amalgamation when using the same foot as partner

Closed Basic Movement (no turn) (LF Chasse may be replaced with a Ronde Chasse. The RF Chasse may be replaced with a Twist Chasse)
Open Basic Movement
Spot or Switch Turns
Three Cha Cha Chas Fwd or Back
Fwd or Bwd Runs
Time Steps (with or without Guapacha timing)
Cuban Breaks or Split Cuban Breaks

The methods of changing feet described are all that are necessary for the theoretical section of the Fellowship examination, although other methods are acceptable in the practical section and for our Gold medal and medallist competitions

METHOD 1   From Open Position to Right Side or Right Shadow Position (Normal opposite foot to same foot as partner)

		Count
	Man and Lady dance 1 - 5 Open Basic Movement	2.3.4&1
	Lady continue with 6 - 10 Open Basic Movement.	(2.3.4&1)
	Man dances his Foot Change as follows	
1	RF back	2
2	Transfer weight to LF	3
3	RF diag fwd	4
4	LF fwd and across, moving towards Lady's L side and turning 1/2 to R, to end LF back and slightly to side in RSP or R Shadow Position	1

Man and Lady now RF back into Man's 6 - 10 of Closed or Open Basic Movement
Follow with any of the listed figures as explained above both commencing with LF. (No hold, R to L hand hold or R Shadow hold)

From Open Position to Tandem Position, Lady behind

As above but Man will step **straight forward RF in line with LF** on 3 & 4 of his Foot Change, to end with LF back in front of Lady. (No hold) Follows as above

FOOT CHANGES (continued)

METHOD 2 **From Right Side or Right Shadow Position to return to Open Position**
(Same foot to normal opposite foot)

Both commence with weight on LF
Man dances the four steps as described for Method 1 (Count 2. 3. 4. 1) while Lady dances 1 - 5 of her Open Basic Movement (Count 2. 3, 4&1)
Continue with 6 - 10 of Open Basic Movement

From Tandem Position to return to Open Position

As above but Man will step **straight forward** on 3 & 4 of his Foot Change to end with LF back. Continue as above

METHOD 3 **From Open Position to Right Side or Right Shadow Position**
(Normal opposite foot to same foot as partner)

		Count
	Man dances 1 - 5 Open Basic Movement then into his Foot Change as follows	2.3.4&1
1	RF back	2
2	Transfer weight to LF	3
3-5	RF Diag Fwd Lock RLR, moving towards Lady's L side	4&1
6	LF fwd and slightly across, towards Lady's L side and turning 1/2 to R, to end LF back and slightly to side in RSP or R Shadow Position	2
7	Close RF to LF without weight (Ball of foot)	3
8-10	RF to side to chasse RLR	4&1

Lady dances a complete Open Basic Movement, then 1 - 5 of her Closed Basic Movement with no turn (Count 2.3.4&1, 2.3.4&1, 2.3.4&1)

Follow with any of the listed figures as explained, both commencing with LF (No hold, R to L hand hold or R Shadow hold)

From Open Position to Tandem Position, Lady behind

As above but Man will move **straight forward** on 3 - 6 of his Foot Change to end with LF back, in front of Lady. (No hold) Follows as above

FOOT CHANGES (continued)

METHOD 4   **From Right Side or Right Shadow Position to return to Open Position**
(Same foot to normal opposite foot)

Man dances the 10 steps as described for Method 3 while Lady dances 1 - 5 of her Open Basic Movement, then 6 - 10 of her Closed Basic Movement
Follow with any figure normally commenced in Open Position

From Tandem Position to return to Open Position

As above but Man will move **straight forward** on 3 - 6 of his Foot Change to end with LF back
Follows as above

Note   The simple Foot Changes as in the Chase (Page 102) may also be used

NOTES